JUSTICE &

CHARITY

JUSTICE &

CHARITY

FULTON J. SHEEN

INTRODUCTION BY PETER HOWARD, S.T.D.

ACS BOOKS

Cover Photograph,
Courtesy of the Diocese of Rochester Archives
Rochester, New York

ISBN 978-1-50510-886-6

ACS Books is an imprint of TAN Books
PO Box 410487
Charlotte, NC 28241
www.TANBooks.com

Printed and bound in the United States of America.

Dedicated to
MARY IMMACULATE
With Filial Homage

Publisher's Note: Fulton J. Sheen's *Justice and Charity* is a series of addresses produced by the National Council of Catholic Men and delivered on "The Catholic Hour" radio program between January and April in 1938.

Period translations of papal documents were used to cite the original text.

This edition is made possible with the permission of The Estate of Fulton J. Sheen/The Society for the Propagation of the Faith. For more information, visit their website at www.onefamilyinmission.org.

Contents

INTRODUCTION

Peter J. Howard, S.T.D.

I n his book *What's Wrong with the World*, G.K. Chesterton made this now famous comment: "The Christian ideal has not been tried and found wanting. It has been found difficult; and left untried." One area of the Christian ideal where these words especially apply is the Catholic Church's social teaching, which has been left untried largely because it is either unfamiliar or ignored outright.

America, and the West, is at a critical crossroad and must decide whether it will follow the Way laid out by Christ and His Church. The alternative is the way of anti-Christ as Jesus said: "He who is not with me is against me, and he who does not gather with me scatters."[1] There is no middle road and it was so important to God that we know *His* road, that He came in the flesh to reveal it to us and then stamped His blueprint into the living memory of His Church, which is His Life mystically prolonged in the world until the end of time.

In this critical moment of history, Providence has placed the following series of conferences by Fulton J. Sheen as a last hope for America and the world to *put on Christ,* who the West has abandoned, and put humanity back on the path of common sense, peace and prosperity.

---

[1] Matt. 12:30.

The following conferences on justice and charity could very well be appended to Fulton Sheen's masterwork *Philosophies at War*, written in the midst of World War II. At the end of his book he wrote:

> The world today is choosing its Absolute. The totalitarian systems have chosen their false gods. The only alternative is the true God. There are only two ideas in all the world. If men do not adore the true Absolute, they will adore a false one. Hitler and others have gone before the world with a New Order—and that it is; new, not only it its politics and economics, but new in its foundation, its religion, its cruelty, its pragmatism and its force. We cannot conquer that New Order by seeking to preserve an Old Order from which it came. The one and only effective means is to build a New Order ourselves—one grounded on the true absolute of God and on His principles of justice and morality.[2]

If we look at where the world is at 80 years later, we see that all but the West seems to have chosen their Absolute. This is what makes them strong and the West weak. And because the West has yet to choose its Absolute, it is being chosen for them. It is a paradoxical absolute of moral relativism that leads to indifferentism and ultimately to totalitarian dictatorship of intolerance in the name of tolerance.

Sheen's conferences on justice and charity are a direct response to this frightening reality. In his customary teaching style, he makes his points clear and simple. And that is how it should be, for God is simple. We should therefore look for simple answers, even when we live in a complex world.

---

[2] Fulton J. Sheen, *Philosophies at War* (New York: Charles Scribner's Sons, 1943).

Fulton Sheen provides a very simple answer to the social inequalities of our times that can be summarized as follows: There is little justice in the world because there is little charity, and there is little charity in the world because there is little God in the world ... because *Deus caritas est*.[3] And within the mystery of God as charity lies the answer to the question of charity (or love of neighbor). Remove God from the equation and there can be no authentic love of neighbor, because there is no love of God whence love comes. In a certain sense, the answer to today's socio-economic ills is that simple. Restore true love and worship of God and you will have true love of neighbor, because you see the good of your neighbor and the good due your neighbor in light of their dignity made in the image of God, Who is love—and not just love, charity, which is connected more to Greek *agape*, which is a divine, sacrificial kind of love.

Sheen's pedagogy was always the same. Begin first with correcting man's way of thinking and soon man will correct his way of living. Sheen was a master metaphysician after his spiritual father, St. Thomas Aquinas. He was obsessed with the question of "What is?" In other words, he was obsessed with understanding the most important question of all "What is reality?", which is another way of asking, "What is the truth?" What is the truth about God, man and creation? How are these three related? Because all reality ultimately points to God as its first cause and final end, all truth is ultimately a theological question: What is God and how do I understand all things *in* God? In other words, answering the *why* of every created thing and every philosophy goes hand in hand with answering the *what* of a particular thing or philosophy.

---

[3] 1 Jn. 4:8.

The greatest tragedy of the modern age is that when it abandoned metaphysics it also abandoned true intellectualism. In other words, it abandoned reason and the common sense that comes with it. The world has unhinged itself from the truth of reality. This was an act of intellectual suicide because it removed reality's only fixed point of reference, God, Who is Truth. Without a fixed point of reference, morality becomes nothing more than an Hegelian dialectic where compromise becomes the general rule of life, a compromised morality that is in constant flux as the two opposing sides of every argument move the new point of reference further and further from reality and truth. History has clearly demonstrated that this cycle of Hegelian dialectical mode of thinking leads to what Pope Benedict XVI called a "dictatorship of relativism". This is what happens when the creature loses its sense or divorces its meaning from its Creator. The meaning and harmony of life becomes blurred and ultimately lost. And when economic and political systems are built upon this philosophy, you end up with the intellectual and moral chaos which pervades the world today.

Fulton Sheen summarizes our modern intellectual crisis with the following words: "The hardest thing to find in the world today is an argument. Because so few are thinking, naturally there are found but few to argue. Prejudice there is in abundance and sentiment too, for these things are born of enthusiasm without the pain of labor. Thinking, on the contrary, is a difficult task; it is the hardest work a man can do—that is perhaps why so few indulge in it."[4]

And this type of society ultimately allows itself to be governed by cheap slogans and catch phrases which Sheen describes as

---

[4] Fulton J. Sheen, "The Decline of Controversy," in *Old Errors and New Labels* (New York: St. Paul's/Alba House, 2007).

"express trains carrying the burden of those who are too lazy to think for themselves".

How did we get to this point?

In order to understand the symptoms of an illness, we must search for its causes. While every disorder can be traced back to Original Sin, our modern philosophical diseases that have led to the greatest injustices ever seen in history have their roots in the French Revolution, which was heralded under the popular slogans of "Liberty, Equality and Fraternity". In the words of the anarchist Prince Kropotkin, written in 1908: "What we learn today from the study of the Great Revolution is that it was the source and origin of all the present communist, anarchist, and socialist conceptions.... Up till now, modern socialism has added absolutely nothing to the ideas that were circulating among the French people between 1789 and 1794, and which it was tried to put into practice in the year II of the Republic. Modern socialism has only systematized those ideas and found arguments in their favor."[5] In other words, the great and terrible revolution of 1789, which dealt the deathblow to the remaining vestiges of Christendom, lives on and grows in every atheistic, totalitarian, anti-human economic and political system in the world today. And like the evils of the French Revolution, every evil committed against humanity by means of these systems is always justified under the alluring, yet undefined and often misleading, banners of "liberty, equality and fraternity".

Under the French Revolution's false trinity of humanistic liberty, equality and fraternity, the twentieth century alone has witnessed the greatest atrocities against humanity the world has ever known. The substitution of absolute Individualism or the Absolute of the State in place of God did not bring about liberty,

---

[5] Nesta Webster, *The French Revolution*, v-vi.

equality or fraternity. Instead, it brought about the greatest account of democide in human history. Over 270 million have been sacrificed on the altars of totalitarianism, Fascism and Communism.

Are nations and governments truly better off without God at their helm?

Americans, especially Christian Americans, will be surprised to learn that most have embraced this false trinity based on humanistic and Hegelian dialectical thinking. This is not difficult to prove. We don't use philosophical phrases like thesis, antithesis and synthesis to describe our ethics today, but we use nebulous words such as "conservative" versus "liberal" and "right" versus "left" to embody the paradigm within which *everyone* must fall. It only takes a cursory look at political history to see that what was considered "conservative" and "liberal" in economics and politics a hundred years ago is not what is considered "conservative" and "liberal" today. For example, what Fulton Sheen describes as Liberalism in 1938 is basically what is considered "conservatism" in 2015.

Into this matrix of Hegelian dialectical reasoning comes Fulton Sheen, who smashes through the lies of this false "Left-Right" paradigm to which America, especially Catholic Americans, has undiscerningly embraced. In response to this grave error, Sheen boldly proclaims a third option that has not yet been considered—and it is not libertarianism. Libertarianism, while recognizing the critical need to defend individual liberty as it applies to government interference, does not, however, seek to define what is the moral criterion that makes man free. This critical limitation of libertarianism will ultimately lead to moral relativism as the tendency of fallen human nature is not virtue, but vice.

The third option which Sheen affirmed is a social philosophy which not only embraces what is good in the desires and tenets of the Left, the Right and the Libertarian, but also offers a means to their practical fulfillment. This option is found in the Church's little-known social teaching on the virtues of justice and charity and their practical application in a system Sheen calls "Distribution".

Distributism is a socio-economic philosophy that found ardent supporters in the great thinkers and prophets for our times such as Hilaire Belloc, G.K. Chesterton, and Fulton Sheen. For that reason alone, it merits our critical attention.

At the heart of Sheen's conferences is his argument that the Church's teaching is not behind the times, but "beyond time," as he liked to put it. Its moral and social teaching has perennial relevance and importance. On this particular issue of justice and charity he draws our attention to insightful teachings of the popes that go right to the heart of addressing the central socio-economic questions of liberty, freedom, capital and social equality, and which practical solution best fulfills them. Sheen never saw the teaching of the Church as mere suggestions, but the very voice of Christ—and a voice we must make heard amidst an increasing anti-Christian world.

> Now this is the authority of the Church and many people wonder, "Why is it we obey the Church?" After all, it's hard to obey some human beings; but they are only the gloves; inside is the hand of Christ. We obey them because they are representatives of Christ. Obeying Christ gives us a tremendous amount of consolation—to have divine truths in those things which concern the soul. For the world, the authority is "they," something anonymous. Everybody follows the styles. Or they say, "Everybody's doing it." Oh, no! Right is right if nobody is right, and wrong is wrong if everybody is wrong. Believe me, in this error infested world we really need a

Church and an authority that is right—not right when the world is right, but one that is right when the world is wrong!"

Throughout these conferences, Fulton Sheen challenges the reader to open his mind to the wisdom of the Church, to think with the Church and put its social and moral teachings into action. It is time for America and the world to wake from its intellectual slumber, and put aside the false paradigms that have led us to our modern moral, social, economic, and political chaos. Modern day prophets like Fulton Sheen call us back to the truth which is only found by a return to God as proclaimed by the prophet Isaiah:

> Seek the LORD while he may be found,
> call upon him while he is near . . .
> Keep justice, and do righteousness,
> for soon my salvation will come,
> and my deliverance be revealed.
> Blessed is the man who does this,
> and the son of man who holds it fast,
> who keeps the sabbath, not profaning it,
> and keeps his hand from doing any evil.[6]

As you read and prayerfully reflect on these insightful conferences of Fulton Sheen, keep the following two points in mind. The first comes from the second President of the United States, John Adams: "Our Constitution was made only for a moral and religious people."[7] These words rang with every clamor of the Liberty Bell as it proclaimed the truths inscribed in the Declaration of Independence, "each man is endowed by their

---

[6] Is. 55:6; 56:1–2.

[7] President John Adams to the Officers of the First Brigade of the Third Division of the Militia of Massachusetts, 1798.1.

Creator with certain inalienable rights of life, liberty and the pursuit of happiness". In other words, our starting point in understanding the words "liberty and justice for all" is, first of all, a declaration of *dependence* on God in Whom life finds its meaning—a God Who personally revealed Himself as Charity: *Deus caritas est.*[8]

The second point is from the prophetic words of Fulton Sheen that carry a greater relevance and urgency now than they did when he first wrote them in 1943:

> We are at the end of an era of history, just as definitely as Rome was at the end of an era when Alaric knocked at its Salarian gates. The difference between that crisis and ours is that in the case of Rome a material civilization was collapsing and a spiritual about to emerge. In the present instance, it is the spiritual which is being submerged and the material which is in the ascendancy.[9]
>
> Our so-called liberal civilization, which is dying, is only a transitional phase between a civilization that once was Christian and one that is anti-Christian. It has no stability of its own, being based for the most part in successive negations of the Christian philosophy of life. It will end either in a return to the Christian tradition or in revulsion against it. This alone constitutes the crisis of democracy; it will either return to its roots or die.[10]

---

[8] 1 Jn. 4:8.

[9] *Philosophies at War*, 172.

[10] *Ibid.*, 173.

THE SPIRIT OF
CHARITY

Address delivered on January 2, 1938

I t is a joy and a privilege to be back with you again. The new series we now inaugurate coincides with the beginning of another year. There are two ways of having a New Year: One way is for time and its calendar to make it "new". This happens whether we like it or not. The other way is for us to make it new by voluntarily infusing it with a new spirit—the spirit of Him Who at this season came to the world to teach us we are sons of God and brothers one of another. It is in the spirit of that same Christ Jesus Our Lord that I wish you a blessed and happy New Year.

Our series this year will be divided into two parts: The first part which will extend from now until Lent will be concerned with the social problem; the second part, from the beginning of Lent until Easter, will be concerned with the individual problem, in particular the problem of suffering in relation to the Cross.

The general title of this series is "Justice and Charity". We choose this title because these two virtues are the only effective cures for two evils: one, the accidental evil of Capitalism, and the other, the essential evil of Communism. Capitalism, on the one hand, with its abuses of concentrated wealth and privilege and its subjection of millions to the lot of insecure wage earners, and Communism, on the other hand, with its class-hatred and revolutionary techniques of bitterness. Capitalism needs principally the virtue of Justice in order that all men may have their due; Communism needs principally the virtue of Charity in order that all may dwell in unity, peace, and concord.

Last November, the Bishops of the United States in the annual meeting of the National Catholic Welfare Conference spoke of these two extremes. The group which forgets justice they described as those who disregard "the social purpose of property" with the result that "selfish interests or private profit rather than social well-being has succeeded in large measure in controlling the policies of governments, in directing finance and industry, and in subjecting labor policies to its own ends." The group which forgets charity, they described as "designing agitators or cunning propagandists whose immediate interest is to create turmoil, bitterness, class conflict, and thus hasten a 'revolutionary situation.'"[1]

The Bishops then go on to say that any discussion or treatment of these evils must be marked by "calmness, accuracy of statements, and prudent restraints."

Firstly, the Bishops recommend "calmness and prudent restraint". This means the treatment of the problem must be concerned not with *personalities*, but with *principles*, not with

---

[1] "For generations the social purpose of property has been too much disregarded and self-interest has increasingly dominated social and economic life. Selfish interests or private profit rather than social well-being has succeeded in large measure in controlling the policies of governments, in directing finance and industry, and in subjecting labor policies to its own ends. Although an essentially disorganizing principle, it has unwarrantably claimed to be the sole organizing force in society, the guarantee of social order, and the cure for social ills. But the half-truths and half-solutions which this extreme individualism has begotten in the social order are now discredited in the minds of thoughtful men." Statement of the Administrative Board, National Catholic Welfare Conference, "Concerning the Christian Attitude on Social Problems," *Catholic Action* (December, 1937).

men, but with *systems*. Secondly, the Bishops recommend "accuracy of statement". This means using first hand authoritative sources on both sides of the question so that the settlement may be on the basis not of prejudice but of reason. In keeping with these two suggestions, we shall never offer a criticism of a system without also offering the constructive program of the Catholic Church, which is unfortunately so little known.

In this opening broadcast we wish to plead for the practice of the virtues of justice and charity. Justice, in order that both sides have a hearing. Charity, in order that when one side is wrong, we rectify the wrong instead of merely halting it.

Too often men approach the social problem by saying: "I am against Labor", or "I am against Capital", or "I hate the bankers", or "I hate the labor racketeers". A statement of that kind is a prejudice; it assumes that the saints are all on one side, and the devils are all on the other. Social Justice does not mean hating the banker, nor hating the union organizer; it means seeking and loving the common good. No one class is always right, whether it be Capital or Labor, because society is not founded upon antagonistic classes, but upon their mutual functioning and correlation for the good of all. A great following could be built up in this country by a vicious attack on labor racketeers, just as a great following could be built up by an equally vicious attack upon capitalists. But to do either is wrong, for it is to forget that a few union racketeers do not make unions wrong, any more than a few evil or unscrupulous capitalists make private property wrong. Our country must not be divided into two extreme classes at one another's throats, each seeking the death of the other; it must be built upon a justice and charity in which our individual rights and privileges are conditioned by the service of the common good. The forces of reaction which would continue the evils of Capitalism can be just as wrong as the forces of anarchy which would pour out the baby with the bath. Let us not be fooled. There *is* a mean between the reaction of those who would retain the wrongs of an older order, and the revolution of those who would totally destroy not only the abuse but even the use of that which is good. Somewhere, thanks to justice and charity, is a golden mean which does not destroy the past with its sacred accumulations of treasured wisdom, or ignore the necessity of a peaceful change for a better future existence. Here are some samples of the Golden Mean between reaction and revolution, as suggested by the Church. One extreme error is that the Capitalist has absolute right to property and all its profits: the other extreme is that of Communism which says that the Capitalist has no right at all to property for all the rights belong to the workers who are entitled to all profits. In between both is the position of the Church which says that neither Capital nor Labor is entitled to all the profits, but both must share in them because both have contributed to their creation.

Or to take another example: For some Capitalists, a wage is just if the worker agrees to accept it, regardless of whether or not it is a living wage; for some labor racketeers, a wage is just if the Capitalist agrees to pay it, regardless of whether his industry can bear it or not. In between these two extremes is the Catholic position that a wage is just when it takes into account "the condition of the business", the "necessities of the workingman and his family", and the "economic welfare of all the people".[2]

This series of talks will not, for the above reasons, appeal either to reactionaries or to the revolutionists: it will seem traitorous to those who want Capitalism condemned as intrinsically wicked;

---

[2] Pius XI, *Quadragesimo Anno*, Encyclical letter on reconstructing the social order, trans. *Five Great Encyclicals* (New York: The Paulist Press, 1939), nos. 71–74.

and it will seem cowardly to those who want to see Labor branded irresponsible. It will be accused by the rich of being anti-Capitalist; it will be accused by the workers of being anti-Labor. It will appeal neither to those who hate bankers nor to those who hate Labor organizers; but we trust it will appeal to identically the same people as those to whom the birth of Our Lord appealed: "to men of good will". In other words, the spirit of our approach will be the Spirit of Justice and Charity, Who was born into our historical order nineteen hundred years ago. His Gospel gives no support to extremists who would exploit Labor or to extremists who would violently dispossess capital. Rather He taught us how to be capitalists without being exploiters, and how to be laborers without being Communists. And how did He show it better than at His Birth, for incidental to the Incarnation was the Union of the Rich and the Poor in the unity of His Divine Person. We must not make the sentimental mistake of thinking of Our Lord as just a Poor Man; He was not just a laborer, nor a proletarian. He was a Rich Person Who became a Poor Man. And this is the description of Him given by St. Paul: "For you know the grace of our LORD Jesus Christ, that being rich he became poor for your sakes; that through his poverty you might become rich".[3] Rich, He was in His Divine nature because He was God, and Lord of heaven and earth. And yet despite that richness He became poor, not only from an economic point of view, but poor principally because He became *man*. That is poverty of the worst kind, because it is limitation. To the eternal confusion of Communists who teach that the rich were made to hate the poor and Labor was made to crush Capital, He came to make both dwell in peace in the unity of His Person. He Who was born poor in a stable could have been born rich in a palace

---

[3] 2 Cor. 8:9.

by the Tiber. Roman legions might have guarded Him at His birth, instead of an ox and an ass. It is this that makes Him the Supreme Reconciler of Capital and Labor, for no one would have expected that He Who made the gold of Caesar's throne would be born on a bed of straw; or that He Who made the warmth of the sun, would be warmed by the breath of oxen; or that He Who owned the earth would be homeless on the earth. Children were born in stables before, but never a Child Who might have been born in a palace. That fact alone makes His history unique. It is no wonder then that the world caught His Spirit, and that the first to come to His crib were the representatives of Capital and Labor—the rich magi and the poor shepherds. There is no record that once there, they engaged in class conflict. Rather they saw the light and two things happened to the greedy rich and the envious poor: the rich lost their avarice for they gave their wealth to the Poor; the poor lost their envy for they learned that there is another wealth than that which the rich men gave away. And on that day the world saw the Golden Mean between reaction and revolution.

As the magi and the shepherds left the crib, the magi realized then, as never before, that the rich need the poor more than the poor need the rich. The destitute need the rich only in order to give them shoes for their feet, clothes for their bodies, a room over their heads, food for their stomachs, and the necessities of a decent normal existence. But the rich need the destitute in order that they might have understanding in their minds, charity in their hearts, and the blessings of God on their lives. As (Jacques-Bénigne) Bossuet has put it: "You rich, make for yourselves friends of the poor; give and you shall receive; cast away your temporal blessings so that you may fill your empty treasure boxes with spiritual ones. This is the only hope left for you; but there *is* that hope. You can receive privileges from their hands, and it is to them that the Holy Ghost sends you that you may obtain the graces bestowed by Heaven".

No more fitting message could be addressed to you at the beginning of a new year than the message to make it new by abandoning hate and class struggle and by living in the spirit of Justice and Charity. Just as the Babe called magi and shepherds to Himself and made the rich and poor kneel in peace beside His crib, so the Church which that Babe founded calls both Capital and Labor to its Communion rail to make them one because they eat the one Bread. Upon no other basis than the justice and charity of religion can enmities be abolished. It is no wonder then that those who most foster class hatred are those who are most opposed to the Babe of Bethlehem. As a Moscow daily puts it: "Christian charity which means kindness to all, even to one's enemies, is the greatest enemy of Communism".[4] We believe that justice is a better remedy than reaction, and that charity is a better solvent than revolution. For that reason we invite all fellow citizens, all Christians, all Catholics, to seek out the solution of our problem in Him Who alone is the model of the rich and the model of the poor, the Exemplar of Capital and the Exemplar of Labor. To neither class does He belong exclusively, for He was neither rich nor poor; He was the Rich Poor Man, and the Poor Rich Man. He was the Rich Person Who voluntarily became a poor man, and therefore the One Who can call both to His Crib and to His Church. As a matter of historical record, He is the only One Who ever walked this earth of ours of whom both the Rich and the Poor, the Masters and the Servants, the Employers and the Employees, the Kings and the Carpenters, the Capitalists and the Laborers can say: He came from *our* ranks; He is *one of our own*.

---

[4] *Pravda* (March 30, 1934).

LIBERTY

Address delivered on January 9, 1938

Today, and the next three Sundays, in a spirit of charity, we shall present the three major social remedies offered for the ills of the modern world, namely, Liberalism, Communism, and Christianity. In order that the presentation might be reduced to its simplest and clearest terms, we shall discuss them in relation to the words so often seen engraved over the public buildings of France since the Revolution: Liberty, Equality, and Fraternity.

The problem is: With which of the three shall we start to reconstruct a new social order? Liberalism says: "Begin with Liberty"; Communism says: "Begin with Equality"; and Christianity says: "Begin with Fraternity". Today, we discuss Liberalism.

By Liberalism we do not mean broadmindedness or progress. Rather by it is meant that system of thought which grew up in the 18th and 19th centuries, and which chose as its primary principle that which the word itself indicates; viz., liberty. By liberty, however, Liberalism did not mean what that word meant traditionally, nor what it means to you and me. Liberty correctly understood is the right to choose between good things in order to develop the highest reaches of our personality. But for Liberalism, liberty was not something *moral*, but rather something *physical*. It meant the right to do, to think, or to say whatever one pleases without any regard for society, tradition, objective standards, or authority. This, as can readily be seen, is not liberty but license. If liberty meant absence of all constraint, as Liberalism said it did, then the policeman who refuses to permit me to drive through a red light is interfering with my liberty, which of course is sheer nonsense.

The three principal tenets of Liberalism were:

I. *The State must not interfere with business.* The function of the State is purely negative, like a policeman. A policeman does not intrude in your daily affairs except to protect you against troublemakers; so too, the State must not interfere with business or the expansion of its markets, the development of its recourses or the establishment of its own code of ethics based on profit, for to do so would be to interfere with and destroy liberty, and anything which interferes with liberty is wrong.

II. *No Collective bargaining!* Liberalism, leaving all things to uncontrolled competition, was opposed to all unions of wage earners. To defend this unsound position, Liberalism argued: "Every man must be left free to make his own contract. But if workers enter a union, and the union bargains for hours and wages, the freedom of the individual to make his own contract is destroyed; and anything which interferes with liberty is wrong."

III. *No interference with the absolute right of property!* Edmund Burke, arguing for Liberalism said: "A magistrate has nothing to do with property; his interference is a violation of the property it is his office to protect." Liberalism asserted that the right to property is absolute; from this it followed that a merchant can not only make as much money as he pleases, but he can do with it whatever he pleases, even ignoring the common good; and the State which dared in any way to control that wealth was accused of destroying liberty; and anything which interferes with liberty is wrong.

Such were the principal tenets of Liberalism.

Now what does the Church think about them? The Church says *all three are wrong.* Let us take up each in detail quoting verbatim from the Encyclicals of Our Holy Fathers Leo XIII and Pius XI.

I. The State is not a policeman as Liberalism holds, neither is it a nurse as Fascism and Communism hold. The State exists for the *common good of all*, and not for the protection of a few privileged interests. As Pius XI and Leo XIII said, "Civil power is more than the mere guardian of law and order.... [I]t is true indeed, that a just freedom of action be left to individual citizens and families; but this principle is only valid as long as the common good is secure and no injustice is entailed".[5] "It is in the power of a ruler to benefit every order of the State, and ... in the highest degree the interests of the poor; and this ... without being exposed to any suspicion of undue interference.... Let it not be feared that solicitude of this kind will injure any interest; on the contrary, it will be to the advantage of all; for it cannot but be good for the commonwealth to secure from misery those on whom it so largely depends".[6]

II. Against Liberalism, which opposed collective bargaining, the Church argues that the workers have a right to organize. The Church frankly told the employers the real reason they were afraid to permit a union was not because they were afraid of violating freedom of contract, but because they were afraid of diminished profits if they had to pay higher wages. "Save the poor workers", wrote Leo XIII, "from the cruelty of grasping speculators, who use human beings as mere instruments for

---

[5] Pius XI, *Quadragesimo Anno*, no. 25.

[6] Leo XIII, *Rerum Novarum*, Encyclical letter on capital and labor, trans. *Five Great Encyclicals* (New York: The Paulist Press, 1939), nos. 26-27.

making money".[7] And as regards the so-called freedom of contract, the Church contended that there is no freedom of contract if the worker has nothing and the employer has everything. With only a hat in his hand and a wife and children to feed he is *forced* under penalty of starving to accept whatever wage is offered him. But by organizing into a union, the workmen would have the force of their united corporate strength to bargain with economic advantages of the employer. "Labor is not a commodity" said the same Pontiff. In order, therefore, to give him real bargaining power the Holy Father pleaded for Labor Unions "so organized and governed as to furnish the best and most suitable means for attaining what is aimed at, that is to say, for helping each individual member to better his condition to the utmost, in body, mind and property".[8]

III. Man has not an absolute control over the use of his property. Liberalism said: "I can earn as much wealth as I please, and I can do with it as I please." The Church answers: "You may accumulate money or property or capital, but you may not do with it whatever you please." And why? Because "the right of property must be distinguished from its use".[9] A man has a right to the wine which he has purchased by his labor, but he may not *use* it as he pleases, for example, to intoxicate himself. "It is idle to contend that the right of ownership and its proper use are bounded by the same limits."[10] So it follows then that the right may not use their wealth as they please; the use of their superfluities is subject to the common good. "No one is

---

[7] *Ibid.*, no. 33.

[8] *Ibid.*, no. 42.

[9] *Quadragesimo Anno*, no. 47.

[10] *Ibid.*

commanded to distribute to others that which is required for his own necessities and those of his household; nor even to give away what is reasonably required to keep up becomingly his condition in life; *for no one ought to live unbecomingly*. But when necessity has been supplied, and one's position fairly considered, it is a duty to give to the indigent out of that which is over. [Of] *that which remaineth give alms*."[11]

Property then is not absolutely owned as Liberalism said, nor is it to be confiscated by the proletariat, as Communism holds. In between the two is the just balance; where, on the one hand, the "natural right ... remains intact" which the "State has no right to abolish", and on the other, the State may "control its use and bring it into harmony with the interests of the public good".[12]

One very important conclusion is to be drawn from the Church's condemnation of Liberalism, namely, we must avoid thinking a change from the present order necessarily means the destruction of liberty. Too often the liberty which the modern man seeks to defend is the liberty of Individualism or Liberalism, which is wrong. In rejecting Communism, too, we must not fall into the error of defending the present order as right in all respects, nor call everyone a Red or a Communist because he is opposed to Liberalism. The Church, which condemns the Communism of today, also condemned the Liberalism of yesterday. Both destroy liberty, but in different ways. Liberalism destroyed liberty by isolating the individual from social responsibilities; Communism and Fascism destroy liberty by enslaving the individual to the will of a Dictator.

The liberty which the Church defends starts with the spiritual nature of man, and not with either the absence of constraint or

---

[11] *Rerum Novarum*, no. 19.

[12] *Quadragesimo Anno*, no. 49.

an identity with the will of the Dictator. Liberty based on the fact that man has a soul is today a deserted shrine, but the Church declares that only when men return to its homage will political and economic peace return. Start with that basic principle, of the spiritual nature of man, and it follows that the State will find its reason for being in securing to its citizens that freedom which is necessary for the perfection of the human personality in its noblest reaches. "Because man is a natural being the state will secure his intellectual liberty; because he is a moral being, the state will protect his freedom of conscience; because he is an economic being, the state will protect his right of association ... because private property is the necessary foundation for individual liberty, it will be defended—nay, if men will it, it shall be restored; ... because the family is the necessary training school of liberty, it will be protected in every possible way; because religion is a necessary discipline for liberty, it will not merely be tolerated, but the freedom of all forms of it which actually serve that end will be scrupulously respected."[13] This is poles apart from the liberty of Liberalism and the slavery of Communism.

The Church refuses absolutely to defend any social order which understands by liberty the right to do or think or say whatever you please without any regard for the common good. As the eye is not free to function unless it inhere in the body and cooperate with it; as the foot is not free to walk unless it recognizes its responsibility and dependence on the organism; so neither is man free to do whatever he wishes with his business unless he recognizes his obligations to society. In fact, the world has been so used to thinking of liberty in terms of private interpretation and absence of constraint, that it has come to regard the necessary emphasis on the social good as

---

[13] Ross Hoffman, *The Will to Freedom* (New York: Sheed and Ward, 1935), 77.

an infringement and violation of its liberty and constitutional rights. It forgets that all political liberties are socially conditioned, simply because John Jones is not only an individual, but also a member of society. In like manner neither a capitalist's right to profits, nor a laborer's right to organize are absolute; they may both be revoked if the common good is ignored, as a man may have his auto license revoked if he drives on his neighbor's lawn.

It was precisely at this point that Liberalism was wrong in the eyes of the Church—it ignored the necessary limitations of liberty, namely the common good of all. The Church refuses to accept as valid the argument of Liberalism which says that under such glorious liberty a ditch digger could become the president of a bank, and a section hand could become the chairman of a great railroad corporation. This is true; but against these isolated cases the Church has always retorted that the few who did rise to such positions of preeminence were no compensation for the millions who did not. It is never a remedy to make slaves into slave-owners, nor is it any consolation for a hundred sheep dying of starvation to know that the hundred and first sheep will live in green pastures. Our economic history reveals quite clearly that Liberalism meant only one thing: the liberty to become unequal, the freedom to die of hunger—for very few tadpoles ever lost their proletarian tails to croak and hump in economic wealth as Capitalistic frogs.

As far back as 1891 the Church warned the world that a false liberty which allowed every man to act as an isolated individual, without any regard for the common good, would produce tremendous inequalities, and particularly two: "Concentration of wealth in the hands of the few" and the appropriation by capital "of excessive advantages ... [claiming] all of the products and profits and [leaving] to the laborer the barest minimum to repair his strength".[14] This is precisely what has happened. The privileged few became stabilized in wealth and the great mass became stabilized in poverty or at best in the condition of wage-earners. Liberalism did one good thing: it did away with *political* inequalities by making all men equal before the law; but it produced tremendous *economic* inequalities, the rich minority and the impoverished majority. It condemned the inequalities of the monarchical past but it glorified the inequalities of the industrial future. In a word, it begot Capitalism, for Capitalism, in a certain sense, is the heir of Liberalism. It is these inequalities Communism hopes to cure. But before considering the Communist solution, which is the elimination of Capitalism as something base, wicked, and seated in iniquity, it remains to ask this important question: What does the Church teach concerning Capitalism? That question will be answered in next Sunday's broadcast.

[14] *Quadragesimo Anno*, no. 54.

CAPITALISM

Address delivered on January 16, 1938

In the last broadcast it was stated that the Church is opposed to any social system which interprets liberty as the right to do whatever you please. Such a system has been historically known as Liberalism. In the economic order it is known as Capitalism, for Capitalism was born of the spirit of Liberalism. Most of us have heard brilliant defenses of it by the vanishing race of "rugged individualists", or raucous and vicious attacks upon it by the Communists. Which is right? Is Capitalism good or bad? What is the attitude of the Catholic Church toward Capitalism?

The Church answers: Define your terms; it depends upon what you understand by Capitalism. Capitalism may mean one of two things. It may mean the private ownership of productive wealth for the sake of profit. In this sense the farmer who owns his land and tills it and then sells his corn and oats for profit, is a capitalist; so is a baker who owns his oven and shop and sells his bread to make money. But Capitalism may also mean something more modern, namely, a system by which great masses of wage-earners are so subject to capital in the hands of a few, that they are able "to divert business and economic activity entirely to [their] own arbitrary will and advantage without any regard for the human dignity of the workers, the social character of economic life, social justice and the common good".[15] Capitalism in

---

[15] *Quadragesimo Anno*, no. 101.

this sense of the term includes not only yesterday's "competitive capitalism" but even today's "monopolistic capitalism" under which "immense power and despotic economic domination is concentrated in the hands of a few".[16]

Now that our terms are defined, let us return to our original question: What is the attitude of the Catholic Church toward Capitalism? The answer is this: If you understand Capitalism in the first sense, as the private ownership of productive wealth for profit, then the Church is not opposed to Capitalism but in favor of it, for there is something good and stable about a society in which the farmer owns his land and the worker has a share in the "ownership, or the management, or the profits" of industry.

But if you understand Capitalism in the second sense, that is, a society in which a minority controls the means of production and claims "all the products and profits and [leaves] to the laborer the barest minimum necessary to repair his strength and to ensure the continuation of his class",[17] then the Church is clearly and undeniably opposed to Capitalism.

But why is the Church opposed to Capitalism in this second sense of the term, the sense in which we shall use it throughout this series of addresses? The Church gives three reasons why it is opposed to such a Capitalism: (1) Because it has concentrated wealth in the hands of the few; (2) because it permits credit to be controlled by a few; and (3) because it leads to a struggle for domination: economic, political, and international.

(1) Capitalism has resulted in the concentration of wealth in the hands of a few, and this concentration of power by these few far exceeds their ownership; more briefly, the few control more than they own. As Pius XI says, "It is patent that in our

---

[16] *Ibid.*, no. 105.

[17] *Ibid.*, no. 54.

days not alone is wealth accumulated, but immense power and despotic economic domination is concentrated in the hands of a few, and that those few are frequently not the owners, but only the trustees and directors of invested funds, who administer them at their good pleasure".[18] A proof of this pontifical critique of Capitalism is that in 1929 only 2,458,049 individuals paid an income tax. In other words only four in every hundred adults earned enough to pay a federal income tax. Ninety-two percent of the people received less than $5000 a year, whereas one-tenth of one percent of the wealthiest families had a total income as large as forty-two percent of the poorest families. In 1929 six million families had incomes of less tan $1000 a year. We choose that year rather than any other because it was the year of our greatest prosperity.

(2) The Church is opposed to Capitalism because as Finance Capitalism it permits credit to be concentrated in the hands of a few banks, thus creating additional servitude and dependence on the part of those who receive credit. As Our Holy Father says, "This power becomes particularly irresistible when exercised by those who, because they hold and control money, are able also to govern credit and determine its allotment, for that reason supplying, so to speak, the life blood to the entire economic body, and grasping, as it were, in their hands the very soul of production, so that no one dare breathe against their will".[19] To be assured that the Holy Father's protest against Capitalism as controlling credit is justified, one need only recall that the Congressional Record of the 72nd Congress reveals that eight banks in New York City in 1923 exercised control of 3,741

---

[18] *Ibid.*, no. 105.

[19] *Ibid.*, no. 106.

distinct corporations, such as insurance, public utility, transportation, manufacturing, and the like.

(3) The Church is opposed to this Finance Capitalism because with its "limitless free competition" it has resulted in a "struggle for domination".[20] This struggle for domination is three-fold: (a) economic, (b) political, and (c) international. (a) "First, there is the struggle for dictatorship in the economic sphere itself"[21]—a statement which is borne out by the fact that in 1933 less than 600 firms owned over one-half of the corporate wealth of the United States. (b) Political domination manifests itself in "the fierce battle to acquire control of the State, so that its resources and authority may be abused in the economic struggle".[22] As far back as 1912 Woodrow Wilson said: "The government of the United States at present is a foster child of the special interests."[23] (c) The international domination is manifested "finally [in] the clash between States themselves", which is imperialism or the desire of economic dictators to extend their markets throughout the world even at the cost of human lives.[24]

Now that the Church has given three reasons why it is opposed to modern Capitalism, it is very much to the point to draw two very important conclusions: (1) The Communists' charge that the Church is the ally of Capitalism is absolutely false. Without any regard for truth, and with no other desire than to incite class hatred, Communism feeds minds on such slogans as the

---

[20] *Ibid.*, nos. 107–108.

[21] *Ibid.*

[22] *Ibid.*

[23] Woodrow Wilson, *The New Freedom: A Call for the Emancipation of the Generous Energies of a People* (New York: Doubleday, Page and Company, 1913), 58.

[24] *Quadragesimo Anno*, no. 108.

Marxian one: "Religion is the opium of the people." The fact is that the Church has never used religion to defend the rich or to put the workingman to sleep, or to make him indifferent either to the ills of Capitalism or the necessities of a decent human existence. Does the above criticism of Capitalism read as if the Church were the ally of Capitalism? Do these words written in 1891 and 1931 to the wealthy read as if the Church were courting their favor because they were wealthy? Leo XIII's encyclical says, "But rich men and masters should remember this—that to exercise pressure for the sake of gain, upon the indigent and destitute, and to make one's profit out of the need of another, is condemned by all laws, human and divine".[25] Not even millions given in charity by capitalists to build libraries and research institutes, to restore old monuments, or to endow hospitals, says the Church (officially), can "take the place of justice unfairly withheld".[26] Going still further the Church teaches: "Neither must it be supposed that solicitude of the Church is so occupied with the spiritual concerns of its children as to neglect their interests temporal and earthly. Its desire is that the poor, for example, should rise above poverty and wretchedness, and should better their condition in life; and for this it strives" always seeking to "save the poor workers from the cruelty of grasping speculators, who use human beings as mere instruments for making money".[27]

When Communism says the Church is the ally of Capitalism, it forgets this very important fact; namely, that there is only one superficial and tiny resemblance between Catholicism and Communism, and that is, both condemn the evils of Capitalism. Instead of the Church being the ally of Capitalism,

---

[25] *Rerum Novarum*, no. 17.

[26] *Quadragesimo Anno*, no. 137.

[27] *Rerum Novarum*, no. 33.

it is Communism which is the ally of the Church in opposing the abuses of Capitalism. In fact the only one *right* thing about Communism is its agreement with religion in its protests against economic injustices. In everything else it is wrong.

When then you hear Communists say the Church is the friend of the Capitalist and the enemy of the workingman, just remember that you will find more solid arguments against the evils of Capitalism in a calm Papal Encyclical, than you will find in a violent red sheet of propaganda; and remember too that the very arguments some Communists are using today against Capitalism are taken from this great Church document, already 47 years old. Compared to the Encyclicals, the Red attacks are but the wild ramblings of men who hate a class which oppresses more than they love a class which is oppressed.

This brings us to our second and final observation concerning the relation of the Church and Communism to Capitalism. Communism says that Capitalism is intrinsically wicked. The Church says: "It is not vicious of its very nature."[28] It is not intrinsically evil because it admits the right to own private property and to utilize it for the sake of profit. But Capitalism may become accidentally wicked by abusing these rights and turning them to the selfish ends of their owners. The Church makes a distinction: between the *right* to a thing and the *use* of the thing.[29] A policeman has a right to his gun, but he may not use it to shoot babes in arms. Communists say, because some policeman abuse the right of their gun, "take all guns away from all policemen and give them to us and we will be your O.G.P.U."[30] The Church says: "deprive only those policemen

---

[28] *Quadragesimo Anno*, no. 101.

[29] *Rerum Novarum*, no. 19.

[30] The "Joint State Political Directorate" was the secret police of the Soviet Union.

of their guns who abuse their right to have one." Capitalism is in need of a social reconstruction but the Church does not believe in destroying its good features, for she most emphatically teaches that the "misuse or even the non-use of ownership [does not] destroy or forfeit the right itself".[31] To put it all very simply, Communism, finding rats in the barn, burns the barn. The Church would drive out the rats.

Furthermore while protesting against these evils in Capitalism, and while pleading to the State to use its power to defend the workingman and the poor, the Church is not blind to the fact that there may be evils on the other side. Listen to these sharp words to labor, whom she is defending: "Religion teaches the laboring man ... to carry out honestly and well all equitable agreements freely made, never to injure capital, nor to outrage the person of an employer; never to employ violence in representing his own cause, nor to engage in riot and disorder; and to have nothing to do with men of evil principles, who work upon the people with artful promises, and raise foolish hopes which usually end in disaster and in repentance when too late."[32]

That is why Communism and Catholicism have two entirely different solutions for the problem of inequality produced by the evils of Capitalism. Communism proposes to solve inequalities by confiscation and dispossession, the Church by legislation and *distribution*. A parable will make it clear.

In a certain rural section of the country there are a dozen farmers selling eggs to a city. Partly by hard work, partly by dishonesty, partly by unjust trade practices, one farmer finally controls practically the whole egg market and the other eleven farmers are reduced to a state where most of them have to work

---

[31] *Quadragesimo Anno*, no. 47.

[32] *Rerum Novarum*, no. 16.

for the monopolist. This inequality in the egg business needs a solution. How do we solve the problem?

The Communist solution is this: An organizer is sent among the eleven farmers inciting them to upset the delivery wagon of the capitalist, then to throw stones at the hens on their nests so that they will not lay eggs, all the while telling the farmers about the big goose eggs which the Socialist hens lay at the command of their beloved Stalin. After the Communist organizer has developed class hatred between one farmer and the other, and in general has disturbed both hens and eggs and their distribution, he then "acting as the vanguard of the masses" seizes all the hens and all the eggs of the twelve farmers. The farmer who owned most of the hens and the eggs naturally resists, but he is "liquidated", which is the Communist word for murder. Two or three of the eleven do not like such violence, and plead against bloodshed; so they are called "fascists" and "trotskyites" and sent to a lumber camp. Then the Communist organizer says to all the farmers who are left: "The problem of equality is solved. You all own equally; there are no more classes, for I am your Dictator and I own all, in the Dictatorship of Eggdom." Then to prove they are equal he makes an omelet out of all their eggs and invites them to dinner.

The Church rejects such a solution because it destroys liberty. The Church contends that not all men like omelets; that some like their eggs boiled, others fried, and others prefer to have them raw. The Church believes in putting the eggs in as many baskets as possible for only when a man is master of the way his eggs are to be cooked, can he be called the maser also of his soul. Communism, on the contrary, puts all the eggs in one basket. Instead of allowing each man to cook his own eggs according to his tastes, it makes an omelet. How poor Communism's omelet is, we shall tell you next Sunday.

EQUALITY

Address delivered on January 23, 1938

How do we begin reconstructing the social order? Liberalism and Capitalism said: Start with liberty, understanding by liberty, absence of constraint. Capitalism had its liberty and it produced unjustified inequalities, the concentration of wealth and power in the hands of a few, and the general impoverishment of the masses. It was only natural for another system to arise offering to heal inequalities by preaching equality. Such is Communism. There is something good about Communism and that is its protest against the injustices begotten by Liberalism. But two very important cautions must be kept in mind. Firstly, Communism is not alone in protesting against injustices; all who believe in virtue—and they are legion—make exactly the same protest. Leo XIII registered a more coherent and objective protest against certain evils of the industrial order than Communism, even with its violent hatred of Capitalism. Secondly, we must not be fooled by believing that because the *protests* of Communism are right, that therefore its *reforms* are right. Cutting off one's head is a remedy for toothache, and so are bad remedies. The proper way to judge a platform is not by its negations, but by its affirmations. Because demagogues say they hate the rich is not a proof that they love the poor; it may only mean that they envy the rich. I can protest against the bad odor of dead lilies without being madly in favor of perfume. If, then, we are to understand the value of Communism as a solution, we must judge it by its reforms.

First we will inquire into the reform of society suggested by Communism; and secondly, show two of its many defects.

In order that there may be no false presentation of the Communist position I shall read from the official *Program of the Communist International*, the third edition of which was printed for the Communists of the United States in February, 1936, and which is distributed by the Workers Library Publishers, New York City. I hold a copy of this official program in my hand and any member of the studio audience who wishes to verify any of the texts may do so after this broadcast. By reading from this official program you will come to know what Communism officially stands for and not what its propagandists would falsely conceal.

The basic argument of Communism is this: Inequalities in the economic order are due to private ownership of productive property which in its turn creates classes in society and makes exploitation possible. Communism proposes to do away with private ownership of productive property as well as the government which supports it, and thus build a classless class.

Let us now ask this official program a series of questions the answers to which will be taken verbatim from the *Program*.

1. Must there be a revolution before Communism can be established and what does it imply?

    Between capitalist society and communist society a period of revolutionary transformation intervenes.... Proletarian revolution, however, signifies the forcible invasion of the proletariat into the domain of property relationships...."[33]

---

[33] *Program of the Communist International* (New York: Workers Library Publishers, 1936), 34–35.

2. What will happen to the Capitalists whom the Communists always call exploiters?

   The characteristic feature of the transition period as a whole, is the ruthless suppression of the resistance of the exploiters...."[34]

3. What will happen to church lands, productive property, industry, transportation, communication services, and big housing property?

   The official program uses the same word in relation to all of them, namely, "confiscation"; e.g., "the confiscation of all property utilized in production belonging to large landed estates, such as buildings, machinery and other inventory, cattle, and enterprises for the manufacture of agricultural products (large flour mills, cheese plants, dairy farms, fruit and vegetable drying plants, etc)".[35]

4. What will happen to the middle classes who are not sympathetic to the Communist revolution and to those who are in favor of landowners.

   The answer is suppression: "The proletariat must neutralize the middle strata of the peasantry and mercilessly suppress the slightest opposition on the part of the village bourgeoisie who ally themselves with the land owners."[36]

5. What will happen to the liberal left-wingers and the intelligentsia who refuse to go the full way of the Communist revolution?

---

[34] *Ibid.*, 36.

[35] *Ibid.*, 40–41.

[36] *Ibid.*, 49.

The *Program* calls for "ruthlessly suppressing every counter-revolutionary action on the part of the hostile sections of the intelligentsia".[37]

6. Why is violence necessarily associated with the Communist revolution?

The *Program* answers: Because it enables Communism to get rid of those who oppose it. Think of how much bloodshed there is hidden in these following lines as the history of Russia has so well proved to be true. "The mass awakening of communist consciousness, the cause of socialism itself, calls for a *mass change of human nature* which can be achieved only in the course of the practical movement, in revolution. Hence, revolution is not only necessary because there is no other way of overthrowing the *ruling* class, but also because, only in the process of revolution is the *overthrowing* class able to purge itself of the dross of the old society and become capable of creating a new society".[38]

7. Finally, what is the official attitude of Communism toward religion?

One of the most important tasks of the cultural revolution affecting the wide masses is the task of systematically and unswervingly combating *religion*—the opium of the people".[39]

8. Does the Communist revolution propose to seize Government power and to overthrow our armies, our police, and our courts?

The *Program* calls for the "violent overthrow". "The conquest of power by the proletariat is the violent overthrow

---

[37] *Ibid.*, 48.

[38] *Ibid.*, 52.

[39] *Ibid.*

of bourgeois power, the destruction of the capitalist state apparatus (bourgeois armies, police, bureaucratic hierarchy, the judiciary, parliaments, etc.)."[40]

If these words were our own, we are sure you would disbelieve them. They sound even unbelievable when you read them in the Communist *Program* itself. That is why before they spring their revolution they have to disguise their real intents and purposes by popular fronts, democratic slogans, and the false face of liberty.

Now that we have presented the reform of Communism in its own words we inquire into its defects. Apart from the chaos which would be occasioned by the revolutionary overthrow of the existing order there are two serious defects among dozens of others in the Communist solution of "equality and the classless class". First, it destroys freedom. Secondly, it does not, as it claims, destroy inequality but on the contrary creates new and worse forms of it.

Firstly, in the language of the Church "Communism ... strips man of his liberty, robs human personality of all of its dignity, and removes all the moral restraints that check the eruptions of blind impulse".[41] As a proof of this statement let us go to the new Soviet Constitution:

(1) Under Communism there is no freedom of confessional liberty, that is, one may not carry on any kind of propaganda for, or defense of, religion, or teach religion to children in groups of over three. This is a denial of religious liberty, and yet such is the effect of Article 124 of the new Russian Constitution, not in so many words but as it has been interpreted by the Soviet

---

[40] *Ibid.*, 36.

[41] Pius XI, *Divini Redemptoris*, Encyclical letter on atheistic communism (Massachusetts: Daughters of St. Paul, 1937), no. 10.

Judiciary. For Article 124 expressly gives to the anti-religious forces the right to propagandize, but it limits the right of the religious forces to that of "worship", that is, to the private exercise of religion alone.

(2) There is no real freedom of press, freedom of speech, or freedom of assembly under Communism, despite article 125 of the Soviet Constitution, because the press belongs to the State and may be used only so as "to strengthen the socialist system." Would we say we had freedom of the press in the United States if every newspaper, radio, and writer had to bolster one of the political parties of the United States and would be declared "an enemy of the people" if he did not? Would we say we possessed freedom if those who dissented with the President were shot without trial? Would we say we possessed freedom if those who dissented with the President were shot without trial? Would we say we had freedom of the press and speech in America if we were permitted to have only one party, and all dissidents who felt there should be another party were killed or sent to a concentration camp where they learned the wisdom of keeping their collective mouths shut? Would we say we had liberty in the United States if the President, within the space of three months, executed the Governors of our (contiguous) 48 States? And yet this is precisely what the beloved Stalin did, for he murdered the heads of every one of the Republics of the Soviet Union in three months. This criticism is true of any totalitarian state, fascist or Communist. The curious fact about it all is that here in America we will allow Communists to attack our President and our Government, a crime for which they would be shot in Russia.

(3) There is only one effective Party allowed in Russia (as admitted by Kalinin, President of the U.S.S.R., on November 23, 1937), namely the Communist Party, and the nomination

of all candidates for election belongs to the Communist Party. Such is the effect of Article 141 of the Soviet Constitution, when read in conjunction with Article 126. This means there is no real freedom of election; the people can in theory choose between candidates of the one Party; they cannot choose between candidates of the one Party; they cannot choose between Parties. In fact they cannot even choose between candidates, for in the last general election there were not more than 30 districts out of 1,143 in which they had more than one candidate from which to choose. The last election in Russia was a shotgun plebiscite and reveals unity of assent to Communism, but a unity under compulsion. A hundred percent electoral victory for Stalin does not demonstrate that everyone believes in Communism. It only demonstrates that Stalin is still strong enough to make his slaves vote for him. Without a choice between recognized opposition all the secret ballots in the world are a farce and are but the dramatized acquiescence in decisions made in the single mind of the Dictator which is much more secret than any ballot box. Add to this the fact that less than 1½% of the entire population of Russia belongs to the Communist Party, which alone possesses the "right to nominate candidates", and you get a true picture of the 1½% of the population dominating the 98½%. This they call "democracy".

(4) There is no freedom to strike in Russia. This may come as a surprise to Americans who are so familiar with the Communist practice of inciting strikes and violence here in America, but the fact is that Article 131, by judicial interpretation, is construed to forbid anyone to strike under penalty of becoming "an enemy of the people". They throw wrenches into everyone else's machine here and subject you to the criminal code if you throw a wrench into one of their own in Russia.

As long as the workers are at the mercy of the Communist Dictator, as long as the Dictator can compel reluctant obedience of the worker by force, terror, O.G.P.U., propaganda, and blood purges, as long as the workers themselves are unable to protest against dictatorship—save at the cost of grave personal injury, imprisonment, or death—as long as they must court the favor of the Dictator by parades, demonstrations, and "long live the workers' friend", as long as they are exiled or shot because they insist on their right to worship God according to the dictates of their consciences—despite all their successful Five-Year Plans, their great army, their new bath-rooms and radios, their new luxuries from night clubs to subways, they can hardly be said to be free! They may all be equal as workers, but so are the prisoners in a work-house! It is better to be poor and free, than to have your stomach full and not be able to call your soul your own. What doth it profit a worker if he has all his material wants satisfied and he cannot protest against a regime which would deny him the spiritual when his day's work is done?

It is quite true that Communism does away with the inequalities of wealth, because the State owns all the means of production; but in their place it has created inequalities of privilege. There are no more Big Bankers, but there are Red Leaders; there are no more Capitalists, but there are Commissars. Communism has done away with the aristocracy of money, but it has not done away with the new aristocracy of privilege. And how could it be otherwise in a regime where *ownership* is distinct from *administration*. Under Communism the *ownership* of the means of production is common, that is, it belongs to the workers; but the *administration* of that ownership resides in the hands of the leaders. Thieves who rob a bank own the loot in common, but the quarrels begin when the ringleaders divide spoils. Then everyone wants to divide. And so it is with

Communism. It begins with the violent confiscation of wealth, but if the leaders were disposed to steal from the Capitalists in the beginning, why should they not be disposed to steal from the workers in the end? The enforced transfer of title to property works no magic in the hearts of men, and can no more revolutionize human behavior than a wearing of a neighbor's hat. Selfishness, injustice, greed are not in *things*, they are in *souls*; and when Communism rejected religion it cut off from itself all possibility of regenerating society. If socializing property did away with injustices we would never hear, as we do, of profiteering by Red Leaders, of profiteering by farm managers, and of raids on the public treasury.

Starting a new order by violent confiscation and murder, as Communists started their new order in Spain, can not make for peace. Can Injustice be the road to Paradise? Can life come from death, love from hate, peace from violence? Confiscating the means of production and socializing them does not do away with the passion for property, any more than the stealing of a man's clothes does away with the shame of nakedness. There is something to be envied under Capitalism, namely, wealth; and there is still something to be envied under Communism, namely, the leader who will have charge of it. Under Capitalism it is personal wealth that produces inequalities, under Communism it is the personal control of that confiscated wealth which produces the new inequalities. The struggle for wealth under Capitalism thus became a struggle for power under Communism. Regardless of how loud one prattles about "comradeship" there has still been found no way of making Communists, once they have wealth in their power, so devoid of the passion of wealth that they will become economic eunuchs, so that the ditch digger will be just as satisfied as the Red Leader.

Communism has been tried and found wanting. It began as Communism, now admits it has not established it, calls its system Socialism, but in fact it is State Capitalism. Thus it is that the system which begins by hating Capitalism takes over all its bad features and ignores its better ones. Communism was right in saying that Capitalism ignored the family rights of the worker, but Communism went one better than Capitalism by destroying the family and making the worker the unit of society. Communism was right in saying that Capitalism reduced the worker to a "hand", but Communism went one better by ignoring his spiritual qualities altogether and treating him as a "stomach" to be fed in order to pile up more wealth for the State. Communism was right in saying that Capitalism ignored the workers' right to share, but Communism ignored not only the worker but the peasant by absorbing them both as employees of the State. Capitalism made the widespread ownership of productive private property difficult, but Communism made it impossible. Communism is Capitalism gone mad; or better still, it is rotted Capitalism. And if you ever want a concrete proof that not even the Communists believe in Communism where it has been tried, just offer to pay their expenses back to the Paradise of Russia in order that they might enjoy its so-called "liberty" and "democracy" and see how many will accept. Not even the Red Leaders in America will go. They prefer to enjoy our liberty in order to destroy it, rather than surrender it to live in the very slavery their own system has created. They know that the whole world has begun to find them out, namely, that Communism is the greatest system ever devised by the human brain to make the rich poor and the poor miserable, but the worst ever devised to make the poor rich and the slaves free.

FRATERNITY

Address delivered on January 30, 1938

How do we solve the social problem? Liberalism and Capitalism answer: "Let every man be free to conduct his business as he pleases." Liberalism and Capitalism had their Liberty and produced only economic slavery and inequality. Communism then suggested a cure for inequalities: "Confiscate all productive private property in the name of the collectivity and everyone will be equal and there will be no more classes." Communism had its Equality and it destroyed Liberty and produced the new inequality of privilege. Now we come to the Catholic solution which says that a reconstruction of the social order must begin not with Liberty, nor with Equality, but with Fraternity.

In order to understand the role of Fraternity take a glance at the present order which needs to be remedied. What is its dominant note? Without any hesitation: Class struggle between Capital and Labor. "Society today still remains in a strained and therefore unstable and uncertain state, being founded on classes with contradictory interests and hence opposed to each other, and consequently prone to enmity and strife."[42] Capital and Labor consider each other as enemies of adversary forces to be conquered; the force of money and influence on the one hand, is too often pitted against the force of mass and organization on

---

[42] *Quadragesimo Anno*, no. 82.

the other. " …[T]he demand and supply of labor divides men on the labor market into two classes, as into two camps, and the bargaining between these parties transforms this labor market into an arena where the two armies are engaged in combat. To this grave disorder, which is leading society to ruin, a remedy must evidently be applied as speedily as possible."[43]

Communism on its own testimony does not attempt to diminish this class-hatred; rather, it attempts to intensify it, until it can, in its own words, succeed in the "violent overthrow of … armies, police, bureaucratic hierarchy, the judiciary, parliaments, etc".[44] This is a queer way indeed to establish industrial peace, and reveals many of the inherent contradictions of Communism. It talks peace but prepares for war; it forbids strikes in Russia but incites them here; it rightly protests against violence directed towards it, and yet insists on the right to use violence against others; it builds a paradise by first making a wreck of the world; it establishes a classless class by throwing classes at one another's throats; it boasts that it does away with two classes and yet establishes in its own country about nineteen classes of privilege; it urges all labor unions to a general strike, but yet "purges" all who would think of it in their fatherland. Its whole system is wrong; you cannot build health in a nation by spreading germs; you cannot educate people by burning the schools; you cannot inaugurate justice by injustice and murder; neither can you do away with classes by intensifying class feeling, nor restore industrial peace by going to war. Let us get this into our heads: We will never have social order by inciting Capital and Labor to violence, any more than we will

---

[43] *Ibid.*, no. 83.

[44] Emile Burns, ed., "Communist Program," *A Handbook of Marxism* (New York: Haskell House Publishers, Ltd., 1935).

have ultimate domestic peace by arming wives with rolling pins to knock all affection out of their husbands' heads and hearts. Increase of darkness is not the way to get light; brotherhood, equality, and friendship among men can no more come out of envy, hate, violence, and "purges" than honesty can come from giving thieves the privilege of stealing. It is just sheer nonsense to say that the evils of Capitalism must get worse and worse before society can get better.

Now for the general principles of the Catholic solution, the details of which must be left to peaceful legislation:

(1) Society is presently organized on the basis of *rights*; the church would reconstruct it on the basis of *function*. At present the word most often used by both Capital and Labor is the word "right". During the past century Capitalism insisted on its "rights" which meant generally the "right of profit". Lately the pendulum has swung to the other extreme where Labor is insisting on its "rights", which to extremists means the right to use violence, and the right to all the profits of industry. This reaction was inevitable. Thus it is that today the so-called "rights" of Capitalism are in conflict with the so-called "rights" of Labor, both of which can be equally intolerant, inhuman, and anti-social.

But how many of us have ever heard Capital or Labor use the word "duty"? How often have Capital or Labor used the words "our responsibility"? How often have both used the words "our mutual obligation"? It is the position of the Church that economic peace can reign only when these words "our mutual obligation"? It is the position of the Church that economic peace can reign only when these words begin to have meaning to the warring parties. The Church says that you cannot have any rights without corresponding duties. But if there are corresponding rights and duties then economic activity has a social character. Then the word "right" gives way to the word "role". This is the

Church's solution, reconstruct society not on selfish "rights" but on the basis of *function*, "binding men together not according to the position they occupy in the labor market, but according to the diverse *functions* which they exercise in society".[45]

Social justice then is not to be identified with hating the Capitalists or hating the labor racketeers, any more than it is to be identified with the selfish rights of either. This is what both Capitalism and Communism forget. The right of the Capitalist to his capital and the right of the laborer to his union, are both conditioned upon the services they render to society; they both require social justification, and they can both be revoked if the common good is not served, just as the right to drive an automobile can be revoked if one refuses to respect the lives of pedestrians or even the lives of jaywalkers.

In order to understand this let us invoke the analogy of the human body. The human body could not function if it were all eyes or all ears. Order is dependent on diverse organs and members working together for the benefit of the whole organism. "Just as in the living organism it is impossible to provide for the good of the whole unless each single part and each individual member is given what it needs for the exercise of its proper functions, so it is impossible to care for the social organism and the good of society as a unit, unless each single part and each individual member ... is supplied with all that is necessary for the exercise of his social functions".[46]

Just as the body is not made up of only body and head so neither is society made up of only Capital and Labor. The body has many organs, for example, the heart to circulate blood, the lung to breathe, the eye to see, etc., and all cooperate for the

---

[45] *Quadragesimo Anno*, no. 83.

[46] *Divini Redemptoris*, no. 51.

good of the whole. In like manner, just as in the human body the various organs do not live by class-hatred and as the eye does not hate the foot because it walks, but all live in harmony by fulfilling their respective functions, so too will society find its peace by uniting its various groups and occupations for the common good. But, there is this difference between the human organism and the social order: A carpenter may become a farmer, and the ditch digger a banker. In order to reveal this free activity of an individual within society as different from the enforced activity of a cell within the body, the Holy Father terms it "vocational"; that is, the individual's social performance may be likened to a vocation.

Instead, then, of organizing society into two camps of Capital and Labor as two enemies with a grudge, society will be organized on the basis of function into various groups or guilds varying in nature and number with the contribution each group makes to society as a whole; that is, "those who practice the same trade or profession … combine into vocational groups".[47]

For example, let there be vocational or occupational groups composed of minters, farmers, textile workers, auto-workers, civil service workers, railroad, telegraph, and telephone men, carpenters, doctors, lawyers, steel workers, and perhaps twenty or thirty other groups depending upon their function in society. Under such an arrangement society is divided not into classes but into professions or vocations. Each group or guild includes not only the organized employees but also the organized employers in the same line of work. The reason for this is that there is a common interest between members of the same trade or profession. Professional and trade groups organize not to show their power or violence against one another, not to intimidate either,

---

[47] *Quadragesimo Anno*, no. 83.

but to settle their corporate differences by peaceful means. The representatives of the employers and the representatives of the employees would, in any given group, for example, the hospital group or the textile group, then form joint boards, meeting in regular sessions for the discussion of all disagreements as well as the promotion of their mutual interests. By such an arrangement classes based on income and wealth would be done away with, and the concept of professions would dominate society. The worker would be elevated from the rank of a passive recipient of salary to that of an effective collaborator endowed with a sense of personal responsibility and dignity.

A society which is divided into Capital and Labor has no real internal unity. The Church's solution gives Labor a unity of common profession, "the bond of union ... provided on the one hand by the common effort of employers and employees of one and the same group joining force to produce goods or give service; on the other hand, by the common good which all groups should unite to promote, each in its own sphere, with friendly harmony".[48]

The Church furthermore suggests that since modern industrial life is extremely complex and one group is dependent upon another group, as the automobile industry is dependent on the steel industry, that there be an interrelation between the various occupational groups. Just as the hand in the human body has one function or profession, and the foot has another function or profession, but both unite for the orderly working of the whole organism, so too the textile group, the auto-group, the farmer group, the banking group, each made up of employers and employees, would work together and direct all their forces and endeavors to a higher end, namely, the good of the whole

[48] *Ibid.*, no. 84.

nation and the betterment of humanity. This would imply the federation of all the groups through representatives into a national council.

A fifth and most important point is the role the State is to play in relation to the professional groups. The position of the Church is clear; it avoids two erroneous extremes, the extreme in which the State has nothing to say, which is Individualism, and the extreme in which the State has everything to say, which is Fascism or Communism. For the functioning of these groups it is important that the State have more to say than it did under Liberalism, and less to say than it does under Fascism or Communism. For Liberalism and the State was a policeman, never daring to interfere with business under penalty of violating its so-called "liberty". For Communism and Fascism the State is a nurse, taking care of individuals and groups from the cradle to the grave and depriving them of their just autonomy and independence. In between these two extremes, of the State being *indifferent* to business, and the State *controlling and managing* business or making it serve "particular political aims" as is the case under Nazism and Fascism, is the golden mean of the State "contributing to the initiation of a better social order".[49] "Let the State watch over these Societies of citizens united together in the exercise of their right; but let it not thrust itself into their peculiar concerns and their organization, for things move and live by the soul within them, and they may be killed by the grasp of a hand from without."[50]

The guild order has no identification with any kind of political order. It will fit into any system and would particularly fit into our own. It will fit perfectly if we avoid the pitfalls of Fascism,

---

[49] *Ibid.*, no. 95.

[50] *Rerum Novarum*, no. 41.

Nazism, and Communism, in which the groups and unions are subservient to the State or the Party. In the Catholic view, the State is the servant of the Catholic groups, not the groups the tools of the State. The Catholic solution avoids the Communist and Fascist evil of putting the majority at the mercy of a dictatorial minority; and likewise the other extreme of Capitalism which puts the majority at the mercy of the minority of greedy economic exploiters.

In brief, the Church's position is this: "the reign of mutual collaboration between justice and charity in social-economic relations can only be achieved by a body of professional and interprofessional organizations, built on solidly Christian foundations, working together to effect, under forms adapted to different places and circumstances," the common good.[51]

The universalism for which the church strives is not that of a class, but of humanity; it unites men, not because they hate Capitalism but because they love justice, not because they are anti-Fascist or anti-Communist or anti-anything, but because they are *Pro-Deo, pro-bono-publico*, for God and country. It respects men and women in our nation, not because they glory in Russia with its purges, but because they glory in America with its freedom.

Justice and Charity—upon these virtues rather than great wealth or great power is the strength of a nation built. Justice there must be to temper the excesses of a false liberty which allowed men to amass wealth without social responsibilities. Charity there must be to mitigate the class hatred which Communists would inflame. But Justice and Charity there cannot be without a firm belief in the God Who judges and the God Who forgives. Upon the recognition of that God our nation

---

[51] *Divini Redemptoris*, no. 54.

was founded and only under that common Father can we call one another "brother". Only when we recognize the God from Whom every grace and blessing come can we understand the symbol of our democracy. It is not a hammer and a sickle, or a swastika, or a bundle of sticks, all of which smack of the earth earthly. It is a bird—not an owl that hoots in the darkness nor a bat that haunts the blackness; not a sparrow that stays close to the earth nor a vulture that thinks only of prey. Rather, with a full consciousness that our rights and our freedom come from beyond the highest mountain and the most distant star, did America choose the symbol of the eagle whose "glory is gazing at the sun".

⚖️
DISTRIBUTION

Address delivered on February 6, 1938

L ast Sunday, a very practical solution for our social ills was suggested, namely, the diminution of class struggle by the formation of professional groups or guilds made up of employers and employees, working together for the common good.

Today, developing the idea of Fraternity, Catholic social teaching offers the second practical solution of the social problem, namely, *Distribution*. We begin with the fact which Communists, Socialists, Fascists, Jews, Protestants, and Catholics, admit in common; that is, the unequal distribution of wealth, its concentration in the hands of the few, and the impoverishment of the masses. There are only three possible ways to remedy this inequality: Firstly, continue Capitalism, in which the man who has nothing must work for the man who has everything, in which the worker is politically free but economically enslaved, and in which the problems of justice are settled by a display of force and civil war, with strikes as the weapon of one army and injunctions the weapon of the other. Or secondly, accept Communism which cures the evil of unequal distribution of wealth by violently confiscating all productive private property, and by overthrowing the government and establishing in its place a dictatorship of the proletariat, such as exists in Russia. Or thirdly, seek distribution of productive private property, which is the Catholic solution, now happily being recognized even by many non-Catholics. Capitalism believes in Possession; Communism believes in Confiscation; the Church believes in Distribution, or the union of popular freedom and economic freedom through widely distributed ownership. More simply, Capitalism stands for Possession through individual selfishness; Communism stands for Dispossession through collective self-ishness; the Church stands for Distribution through Charity and Justice.

Apart too, from the disruption of society by violence and revolution, the break with tradition, the surrender of liberty to a dictator, Communism forgets that, as Aristotle said centuries ago, "that which is the business of everyone is the business of no one". Under Communism the factory belongs to the workers in the same way the public parks belong to us. And yet how many Americans do you see going into the parks to pick up refuse on Monday morning, or mending a hole in the pavement? Production for profit such as exists in democratic countries can be made compatible with freedom and responsi-bility. Russia has proved that production for us cannot be made compatible with freedom, for when you get a few bureaucrats deciding how many pairs of trousers have to be made for the workers, you very soon reach the condition described by the Commissar of the Food Industry in Russia, Mikoyan, who said, "We are accustomed in the Soviet Republic to have only goods of bad quality and always in insufficient quantities".[52] Freedom leaves when everything, even the food you eat, is planned for you by someone else. Anyone with ideas of his own is just as much a nuisance to a planned economy as to an army at war. When the dictatorship of the proletariat is set up, to whom do

---

[52] Statement made at the Plenary Session of the Central Committee of the Communist Party, *Izvestia*, (Dec. 27, 1935); cf. *Pravda* (July 31, 1936).

the proletariat dictate? And what happens if a worker hold an opinion contrary to the Dictator? The answer is: He is "liquidated" or "purged" or sometimes he just "disappears". To dictate to a Dictator is the shortest cut to a tombstone.

Contrary to Communist propaganda, which tells us that the world must choose between Capitalism and Communism, the Church insists there is a third choice and a golden mean, namely, the wider diffusion of private property, both productive and consumable.

But the Church looks beyond even the payment of a living wage. Here we hit upon the very essence of the Catholic solution. "In the present state of human society.... We deem it advisable that the wage contract should, when possible, be modified somewhat by a contract of partnership.... In this way wage-earners are made sharers in some sort in the ownership, or the management, or the profits" of industry.[53]

The argument the Church urges for a modification of the wage system by giving the proletariat some capital reveals a principle which the modern world has completely forgotten, namely that "hired labor" has a "social as well as personal or individual aspect".[54] It has an *individual* character because it is personally performed through moral duty or necessity. Labor has also a *social* character. This is particularly evident when a man hires himself out to labor for another. The social character of his labor is there revealed by the fact that he is part of an order in which "brains, capital, and labor combine together for common effort"; his labor is social also because he is a member of society.[55] Furthermore, the succession of his laboring days,

---

[53] *Quadragesimo Anno*, no. 65.

[54] *Ibid.*, no. 69.

[55] *Ibid.*

the raising of a family for society, the education of children for the next generation, all constitute a social contribution.

Now what return does the worker receive for his labor? For his individual contribution the worker receives wages, with the twin fears of unemployment and insecurity. But what does he receive for his social contribution, his constantly increasing contribution to the common good and his constantly deteriorating physical strength? Presently, except in a few instances, he receives nothing. Wages recompense him for his hours by the clock, but they do not recompense him for the new wealth that is created by him in cooperation with "brains and capital". That is where the suggestion of the Holy Father comes in: the worker should be entitled to some share in "the ownership, or the management, or the profits" of industry. In other words, since he makes a social contribution he should also receive a social reward. The Church avoids the two extremes of Capitalism and Communism. Capitalism says the capitalist may "claim all the profits" while the worker has a right solely to his wage, which is often an injustice to the worker. Communism, going to the opposite extreme, would say that the worker had the right to the whole product, which would be an injustice to the one who owned capital. "Such men, vehemently incensed against the violation of justice by capitalists, go too far in vindicating the one right of which they are conscious."[56] The Church says neither class must be excluded from a share in the profits. "Wealth ... must be so distributed amongst the various individuals and classes of society that the common good of all ... thereby promoted ... [for] the vast differences between the few who hold excessive

---

[56] *Ibid.*, no. 57.

wealth and the many who live in destitution constitute a grave evil in modern society."[57]

The next question is how and why should it be done? How will this be done? By violence? No! By confiscation? No! By educating the employer? Yes! By law? Yes! "The law should favor ownership and its policy should be to induce as many as possible to become owners."[58] This is a call to give the workers not only personal private consumable property, but even productive property.

Why should it be done? Because from a wider distribution of property three benefits would follow:

1) It would diminish class hatred and the "gulf between vast wealth and deep poverty will be bridged over, and the two [classes] will be brought nearer together".[59]

2) There will be "great abundance of the fruits of the earth. Men always work harder and more readily when they work on that which is their own.... Such a spirit of willing labor would add … to the wealth of the community".[60]

3) It would make people more patriotic for "men would cling to the country in which they were born; for no one would exchange his country for a foreign land if his own afforded him the means of living a tolerable and happy life".[61]

For the Catholic, then, the defense of the present system of Capitalism in which wealth is in the hands of a few is almost as wrong as the Communist solution which would destroy that

---

[57] *Ibid.*, nos. 57–58.

[58] *Rerum Novarum*, no. 35.

[59] *Ibid.*

[60] *Ibid.*

[61] *Ibid.*

wealth and expropriate it all into the hands of the Red Leaders. The Communists want to "break up" Capitalism, by making the State capitalistic, and the workers proletarians or wage earners; the Church wants to "break down" Capitalism by making the workers share "in the ownership, or the management, or the profits" of industry. The Communists want to concentrate; the Church wants to distribute.

The Church does not believe in putting all the eggs in one basket, but in giving a man a right to own a few eggs and, if he wants, to raise chickens and thus become a Capitalist himself. By distributing a wide mass of property-owners throughout the country with their scattered powers, privileges, and responsibilities, one creates the greatest resistance in the world to tyranny, either political or economic, and also to foreign propaganda, either Fascist or Communist. Man likes liberty, likes to extend his personality by ownership, likes to call things his own, likes certain kinds of local affection, and these things the church proposes to give him.

When the Church holds for a worker sharing in the wealth he produces, it does not propose mathematically equal distribution, but a sufficient distribution to give a tone and a spirit to society. Neither does the Church mean a return to small craftsmanship, for ownership of small things and distribution of ownership are not identical. At the present time many a worker is not economically free because he lacks a possession to which he can give the imprint of his own will. To have his life ordered by others, who have no other authority than that they own the place where he works, is not freedom. That is why Capitalism will not do. Neither will a mere sharing the wealth in the hands of the State do, for what is the use of sharing the wealth unless you have something to say about it? It is not shared wealth workers want—for workers who receive wealth because the State sees that they do are slaves. If the State withdraws its patronage they are left with nothing. There is very little difference between a worker losing his job because a Capitalist discharges him and a worker losing his job because a Commissar liquidates him—except that in the former case he still has his life. Self-government and responsibility, which are the attributes of freedom, are impossible when the Capitalists own all or when the Red Leaders own all.

In between these two extremes of Capitalism and Communism is a reconstructed order which secures the political and economic freedom of the worker. To the great credit of some modern industrialists these pleas of Leo XIII and Pius XI are already being put into practice, and the workers are being given some share in the profits they helped to create. The president of one corporation set up an irrevocable trust fund of $250,000 (one-half of his personal fortune) invested in 7% cumulative stock of his company, the returns of which are to be paid to his workers, and this after increasing the salaries of 350 workers $85,000 a year. Another industrialist offered $1500 worth of stock to each of his employees, gave them the right to elect three directors to the corporation's board of eight, and assured them that first dividends would be paid to employee stockholders.

There is a golden mean between selfishness and dispossession and that is sharing and distribution. Such is the Catholic solution, and it is one which will demand sacrifices which, up to the present, the majority of Capitalists have been unprepared to make. Either big business in this country will share the profits with the workers as the Church asks, or it will be in danger of having its business confiscated by violent hands. There is no other course. Either they will give freely, or they will surrender involuntarily. Why should the employer monopolize for themselves tremendous reserves for depreciation, and give themselves vast bonuses, and yet make little or not provision for the social contribution of the employees who helped to create that wealth? "Social justice cannot be said to have been satisfied as long as workingmen are denied ... the opportunity of acquiring a modest fortune and forestalling the plague of universal pauperism; as long as they cannot make suitable provision through public or private insurance for old age, for periods of illness and unemployment".[62]

The Church is not opposed to Communism only because it is anti-religious and anti-God, or because it is violent, revolutionary, and disruptive of culture. The Church is opposed to Communism also because it enslaves the worker by keeping his body and soul chained to a Dictator: his body chained because the Dictator has all the jobs; his soul chained because he must think what the Dictator thinks. Furthermore, the Church believes that one of the greatest obstacles in the way of effectively combating the evils of Communism is "the foolhardiness of those who neglect to remove or modify such conditions as exasperate the minds of the people, and so prepare the way for the overthrow and ruin of the social order".[63] Remove the environment in which Communism grows and you do much to remove the menace of Communism. But if our great industrialists would sit down with their heads between their hands, read over these encyclicals of the Holy Father, and then announce their dividends not only on the financial pages of our newspapers, but also on the bulletin boards of their factories; if they would make their laborers "sharers ... in the ownership, or the management, or the profits",[64] as the Encyclical asks, then they

---

[62] *Divini Redemptoris*, no. 52.

[63] *Quadragesimo Anno*, no. 112.

[64] *Ibid.*, no. 65.

would need to worry less about the Reds. And the Communists know this; they admit that it is difficult for Communism to grow where business conditions are just. As their own official International Press Correspondence states: "the radicalization of the workers and their increasing impoverishment is the best soil for Communism."[65] That means they want to see the workers kept in a lowly and unjust condition, for then they can incite them to violence. But share the wealth with the workers, help them to become owners and sharers in the industry or factory or business where they work, and they will think twice before they follow the Communist cry for violence. They will see that they would not be destroying *your* property alone but *theirs* also. They will "sit down" on your machines, but they will not sit down on their own. Then the Communist will no longer be able to incite hatred against Capitalists, for the workers will be Capitalists themselves, that is, owners of the productive Capital which the Communists would seize. Then we shall see an industrial order in which 20,000 men will not say, for example, "we are working *for* such and such a corporation", but "we are working *with* the corporation".

With this we come to the end of the triad: Liberty, Equality, and Fraternity. A social order cannot be constructed on liberty, understood as the absence of constraint, for this means in practice the right of the strong to devour the weak, as the evils of Capitalism have so well proved.

Neither can a social order be constructed on the basis of Equality, understood in the economic sense of the term, for this assumes that because men share wealth they are all equal. Thieves share the same loot, but they are not equal with those who do not steal. This false equality of Communism destroys freedom,

---

[65] August 10, 1935.

because it identifies it with willing whatever the Dictator wills, and in the end creates a worse aristocracy than that of wealth, namely the aristocracy of "careerists" who ride to luxury on the wild horse of confiscation, violence, and privilege.

A true social order can be built only on the basis of Fraternity; namely, one inspired not by the profit-motive, which is Capitalism, not by the political-motive which is Fascism; not by the violence-motive which is Communism—but by the love-motive which is Christianity. Start with fraternity, which means that all men are brothers under the Fatherhood of God, that all must function for the common good of society and for the peace of the world, and liberty and equality will follow. Liberty will follow, for the masses will then be free from economic want which will leave their souls free to seek that higher destiny to which they are called, as heirs to the glorious liberty of the children of God. Equality will follow, for all men will be equal in the possession of the inalienable and sacred rights of human personality which no Dictator can take away, and equal also in their right to share the common heritages of civilization. Gone then will be that false equality of Communism which will tolerate no hierarchy. False because equality implies multiplicity in unity; gone will be that false liberty of Liberalism which is but another name for selfishness. In its place will come the equality which admits of differences and the organic relations of part to part for the proper functioning of the whole, and the real freedom which will be powerful enough to enforce freedom. Establish a society of that kind on the basis not of hate but of charity and men will salute one another on the streets not by the atomic name of "Comrade" but by the Christian name of "Brother".

THE TROJAN HORSE

Address delivered on February 13, 1938

The Holy Father in his letter on Atheistic Communism sounds this warning note concerning the tactics of Communism: "In the beginning Communism showed itself for what it was in all its perversity; but very soon it found it was thus alienating the people. It has therefore changed its tactics, and strives to entice the multitudes by trickery of various forms, hiding its real designs behind ideas that in themselves are good and attractive ... they carry their hypocrisy so far as to encourage the belief that Communism, in countries where faith and culture are more strongly entrenched, will assume another and much milder form. It will not interfere with the practice of religion. It will respect liberty of conscience.... See to it, Venerable Brethren, that the Faithful do not allow themselves to be deceived! Communism is intrinsically wrong, and no one who would save Christian civilization may collaborate with it in any undertaking whatsoever. Those who permit themselves to be deceived into lending their aid towards the triumph of Communism in their own country, will be the first to fall victims of their error."[66]

This indictment of Communism is neither too severe nor unjust, for everything the Holy Father says about Communistic methods, Communism itself admits. In order to prove this point,

---

[66] *Divini Redemptoris*, no. 58.

every reference in the course of this broadcast will be taken only from Communist sources. The point to be proved is this: Communism has changed its tactics, but not its end or purpose; namely, the revolutionary overthrow of the existing order.

When Communism began in Russia in 1917 it was generally expected that within a few years the whole of Europe would be in the throes of a Communistic revolution. For that reason, Moscow instructed its delegates in various part of the world openly to preach revolution and practice violence. But the world, quickly seeing that paradises are not built by bloodshed, reacted against the violence of Communism and defeated it. Russia finally recognized this fact and in July and August of 1935 it called the Seventh World Congress of Communism which decided to change the tactics of Communism. From that point on it resolved to use non-revolutionary language in the open to attain revolutionary ends in secret.

Without openly admitting that the world would not have a revolution simply because Russia had had one, the Seventh World Congress now decided its former tactics were wrong. The world was not yet ready for revolution, conditions were not the same elsewhere as in Europe, and the majority of mankind still believed the best way to heal social ills was by legislation and not by revolution.

To accommodate themselves to the modern mentality the Communists decided to cease talking revolution and to begin talking "democracy", "peace", and "hatred of Fascism". Their new program called for a "United Front" with all groups, parties, and programs, on the broadest possible basis of unity. The new method was very much like that of the card shark who makes friends with his victim on the "United Front" ground that they both like a drink. The innocent victim does not yet know what the card shark intends to do, but the card shark knows. The affability and the willingness to pay for the drinks, the sleek geniality, are all details of his "front" and a part of his tactics.

The United Front of Communism is in like manner the fake face of Communism. During the period of the United or Popular Front, Communism says nothing about the destruction of private property, nothing about the hatred of religion, nothing about Lenin's statement "killing is no murder".[67] On the contrary, it speaks of its love of America, the rights of the worker, its sympathy for religion, and its passion for democracy.

Does this mean Communism has changed its philosophy or that it has given up its intention to overthrow the existing order? No! It only means it has decided not to talk about those things *yet*. The time is not ripe for the kill. It has merely changed its tactics, but not its principles. To put it all very simply, the United or Popular Front is only a technique of the moment, like the card shark's paying for the drinks. That this is the plain truth we know from the General Secretary of the Communist Party in the United States who writes in his book, *What is Communism*: "We must emphasize that this united front government would be a transitional form ... [for the] masses ... not yet prepared to fight for *Soviet Power*".[68]

In the Gospel language this means the United Front is the wolf in the clothing of sheep. These words are nothing else but the echo of the official *Program of the Communist International*, which dictates the methods to be used during what it calls the pre-revolutionary period.

As this official program puts it, "Throughout *the entire pre-revolutionary period* a most important basic part of the tactics of the Communist parties is the *tactic of the united front*,

---

[67] Hill and Mudie, eds., "Letters of Lenin", *Iskra*, no. 20.

[68] *Ibid.*, 99.

as a means towards most successful struggle against capital, towards the class mobilization of the masses and the exposure and isolation of the reformist leaders".[69] "When there is no revolutionary upsurge, the Communist Parties must advance *partial* slogans and demands that correspond to the every-day needs of the toilers, linking them up with the fundamental tasks of the Communist International" of Moscow.[70] "The Party determines its slogans and methods of struggle in accordance with … circumstances, with the view to organizing and mobilizing the masses on the broadest possible scale…. This it does by carrying on propaganda in favor of increasingly radical transitional slogans …[and] this mass action includes: a combination of strikes and demonstrations … and finally, the general strike conjointly with armed insurrection against the state power".[71]

Let us analyze these statements. Communism changes its tactics; it no longer talks revolution, it talks against Fascism; it no longer talks arms, it preaches peace; it no longer talks about overthrowing government, it talks about preserving democracy; it no longer talks about butchering the Capitalists, it talks about the rights of the worker. In other words, it has changed its complexion, but has it changed its face? It changes its tactics, but does it change its desire for revolution? It changes its talk, but does it change its mind? It has merely decided that the best way to achieve revolution is not to talk about it, but to work secretly for it. The termites who eat away your porch do not first ring your door bell, inform you of their presence, and tell you they propose to make the roof fall on your head. They seem to know they can accomplish more by the "United Front"

---

[69] *Communist Program*, 82.

[70] *Ibid.*, 81.

[71] *Ibid.*, 80.

tactics of boring secretly from within. You know they have been at work only when the roof falls upon your head.

Is such the new tactic of Communism? Communists admit that it is, only instead of using the example of termites to explain their new approach they use the example of the Trojan Horse. The exact words of the George Dimitrov to the assembled delegates of the World Communists at the Moscow Congress, among whom was the Communist candidate for President of the United States in the last election, are these: "Comrades, you remember the ancient tale of the capture of Troy. Troy was inaccessible to the armies attacking her, thanks to her impregnable walls. And the attacking army after suffering many sacrifices, was unable to achieve victory until with the aid of the famous Trojan horse it managed to penetrate to the very heart of the enemy's camp."[72] In that large wooden horse were hidden soldiers whom the defenders of Troy never suspected of being on the inside, until they arose to seize power. In like manner Communists are urged to wheel their Trojan Horse into our labor unions, religious organizations, political parties, athletic associations under the guise of a peaceful United Front, until they can tear off their mask and throw this country into a barbarous Civil War such as they instigated in Spain, so that they may emerge victorious and thus honor their beloved Comrade Stalin. Their United and Popular Fronts call for a union of Communists with other political organizations, but what these political organizations forget is that Communism uses them only to further its revolutionary ends. Listen to this Official Resolution of the Communist International of August 20, 1935: "The unification of social-democratic parties, in any

---

[72] Georgi Michajlov Dimitrov, *The Working Class Unity: Bulwark Against Fascism* (New York: Worker's Library, 1935), 52.

particular organization with the Communist Party, should be subject to the recognition of the necessity of the revolutionary overthrow of the existing order, and the installation of the Dictatorship of the proletariat under the form of the Soviets."[73]

This means it would be well for Americans to suspect all political parties who accept the support of the Communists, for on their own admission, the Communist union with these parties is "subject to the revolutionary overthrow of existing society".

But this is not all. Lest anyone should still believe that their seemingly peaceful tactics means anything less than revolution, let us hear a word from their own leader. D.Z. Manuilsky summarizing the Congress states: "Tactics, generally may change, but the general line of the Communist International ... *for the proletarian revolution* ... remains unchanged."[74] On a preceding page, the same Bolshevik also states that the "Communists must actively intervene in the present mass movement and strive to raise it to ... the revolutionary overthrow of capitalism and the establishment of the proletarian dictatorship".[75] Furthermore, Dimitrov said that Communism had "intentionally expunged from the reports as well as from the decisions of the Congress *high-sounding phrases* on the revolutionary perspective".[76] But he goes on immediately to warn us that they still believe in revolution. "We did this not because we have any ground for appraising the tempo of revolutionary development less optimistically than before." Then he concludes that by using the

[73] *Pravda* (August 6, 1935); cf. Chap. 6, *Resolutions* (Aug. 20, 1935).

[74] Dmitriy Manuilsky, *The Work of the Seventh Congress of the Communist International* (Moscow, Leningrad: Co-operative Pub. Society of Foreign Workers in the U.S.S.R., 1935), 65.

[75] *Ibid.*, 63.

[76] *The Working Class Unity: Bulwark Against Fascism*, 165.

new tactics which he advocates, they will be doing everything to "accelerate more than in any other way, the creation of the subjective preconditions necessary for the victory of the proletarian revolution".[77]

Now, what kind of revolution do they propose to carry on? Will it be one in which there will be a dictatorship and the abolition of landed private property? The answer of the *Program* is, Yes: "In carrying out all these tasks of the dictatorship of the proletariat, the following [postulate] must be borne in mind: the complete abolition of private property in land...."[78]

Will the revolution mean the purging of those who oppose the revolution as it does in Russia, and as it did in Spain?

The answer of the *Communist Program* is, Yes: "The violence of the bourgeoisie can be suppressed only by the stern violence of the proletariat." "The characteristic feature of the transition period as a whole, is the ruthless suppression of ... resistance."[79] Again, we read in the *Program* of "ruthlessly suppressing every counter-revolutionary action on the part of hostile sections of the intelligentsia",[80] and of "mercilessly [suppressing] the slightest opposition on the part of the village bourgeoisie".[81] This gives an indication of how sincere the Communists are when they talk of democracy. Democracy means, to us, the right to dissent. To them it means the right only to say "yes" to the will of the dictator.

---

[77] *Ibid.*

[78] *Communist Program*, 44.

[79] *Ibid.*, 36.

[80] *Ibid.*, 48.

[81] *Ibid.*, 49.

Does the revolution mean that our government, our courts, our armies, and our police will be suppressed? The answer is, Yes. "The conquest of power by the proletariat is the violent overthrow of bourgeois power, the destruction of the capitalist state apparatus (bourgeois armies, police, bureaucratic hierarchy, the judiciary, parliaments, etc.), and substituting in its place new organs of proletarian power, to serve primarily as instruments for the suppression of the exploiters."[82]

Does the Communist Revolution imply that during the revolution those who oppose it will be purged in the Stalin fashion? The answer is, Yes: "Revolution is not only necessary because there is no other way of overthrowing the *ruling* class, but also because, only in the process of revolution is the *overthrowing* class able to purge itself of the dross of the old society...."[83]

Finally, does the Communist Revolution mean the persecution of religion? The answer is, Yes. "One of the most important tasks of the cultural revolution affecting the wide masses is the task of systematically and unswervingly combating *religion*—the opium of the people."[84]

And if you doubt their revolutionary intentions in America then let me read the Communist testimony before a special committee of the United States House of Representatives, 71st Congress, Report No. 2290. The present Chairman of the Communist Party of the United States who arrived back in America after attending the Communist Congress in France and visiting Communist headquarters in Moscow, is being questioned by the government.

---

[82] *Ibid.*, 36–37.

[83] *Ibid.*, 52.

[84] *Ibid.*, 53.

Q. ...the workers in this country look upon the Soviet Union as their country, is that right?

A. The more advanced workers do.

Q. Look upon the Soviet Union as their country?

A. Yes.

Q. They look upon the Soviet flag as their flag?

A. The workers of this country ... have only one flag and that is the red flag...

Q. ...are the Communists in this country opposed to our Republican form of government?

A. The Capitalist democracy—most assuredly...

Q. And they desire to overthrow it through revolutionary methods?

A. I would like to read from the program of the Communist International.... The conquest of power by the proletariat does not mean peaceful capturing ... by means of a parliamentary majority ... the violence of the bourgeoisie can only be suppressed by the stern violence of the proletariat.

Q. You take your orders from the Third International, do you?

A. ...The Communist International is a world party, based upon the mass parties in the respective countries. It works out its policy by the mass principles of these parties in all its deliberations ... when a decision is arrived at ... the workers, with their customary sense of proletarian discipline, accept [it] and put [it] into effect.

Q. Do the Communists in this country advocate world revolution?

A. Yes...

My friends, if this be not disloyalty—then let us burn our dictionaries! If this be red-baiting, then tell me where lies America's right to self-preservation. Is the doctor who takes out a ruptured appendix an appendix-baiter? Is the judge who sentences a murderer to prison a criminal-baiter? Is the father who defends his wife and children from a burglar's violence a burglar-baiter?

Be not deceived then by the Communists draping themselves in the American flag and, with tears in their eyes, protesting their love of America—just remember that last fall 3000 of them in Madison Square Garden raised their clenched fists and with shrill voices pledged themselves to the establishment of "Soviet America".

If you love America you should just as much resent that pledge as if 3000 Fascists pledged themselves for a "Fascist America".

Be not deceived then by the anti-Fascist front of Communism. Just remember that Communism is Soviet Fascism, and, as a loyal American, if the Communists ask you to join the "American League against War and Fascism" (now called, euphemistically, the American League for Peace and Democracy), tell them you will join it if they will make it an "American League against War, Fascism, *and Communism*".

Be not deceived by the Communists' present tactics of ceasing to be roaring lions and appearing to be cooing doves. The American Communist Party is a member of the International Communist Party of Moscow. That is why the Communists of America will neither deny their revolutionary intentions, nor affirm them. They will not deny them because if they did Moscow would not tolerate them one minute; they will not affirm them because if they did America would not tolerate them one second.

That is why Communism is the greatest humbug ever foisted on the American people.

That is why the Holy Father has warned us not to be deceived by their hypocrisy about religion and democracy and their love of the workers. Our attitude toward their extended hand has been well expressed by M. Le Cour Grandmaison of the French Parliament who said to the Communists: "If the hand you hold out to us is that of the starving, we will give you brad both of body and soul; if that of the wounded, we will bear on our shoulders this fraternal sorrow; if that of the blind, we will guide you towards the light; if that of the despairing disinherited, we will give you peace, joy, hope and love; but if the hand that you offer is that of the traitor, of the seducer, of the enemy of souls, then in the name of Christ who saved our souls with His Blood we will reject your gesture."[85]

The tactics are designed solely to deceive. They will fool a few of our countrymen, but very few. Americans love the honest man; that is why they have no fear of the sword. But they dislike the deceiver, the knave, the one who conquers by stealth. These very tactics Communism is using now were used centuries ago, when a nervous man twitching nervously at a money bag, stole down a Jerusalem hillside. Crossing a brook, he turned to his followers and said: "Whomever I shall kiss, that is he; lay hold on him."[86] And Judas then threw his arms about the neck of Our Blessed Lord and blistered His lips with a kiss. Why did he use the kiss? Because he knew there was something so Divine and Sacred about Our Blessed Lord that He could be overcome only by some mark of affection.

---

[85] *The London Universe* (Feb. 4, 1938).

[86] Mark 14:44.

In like manner, why does Communism use the kiss of the United Front? Why do they use the kiss of the "tactics"? Because they know there is something so God-given and so sacred about our national institutions that they must preface their overthrow with some sign of love. They know some things are so good that they can be betrayed only by a good sign—so they blister our national cheek with a kiss.

It is just that kiss that made Judas the most ignominious man in human history, and it is his direct descendants who turn our blood cold. Their tactics, deceits, and ruses to gain wicked ends, revolt all noble hearts and honest minds. If then you know the tactics of Communism, you can hear its promises, peruse its propaganda, attend its inflammatory sessions, glance into its anti-religious museums, scan its atheistic literature, read its hymns of hate against God and fellowman, and you will never once be convinced that there is no God. If you know its tactics, you will however be convinced of one thing, and that is, that there is a Devil!

PATRIOTISM

Address delivered on February 20, 1938

The treatise on Patriotism in the writings of the greatest philosopher of all times, St. Thomas Aquinas, is to be found under the subject of "Piety". This at first may strike as strange those who think of piety as pertaining only to love of God. But once it is remembered that love of neighbor is inseparable from love of God, it is seen that love of our fellow citizens is a form of piety. In these days when so many subversive activities are at work, a reminder of the necessity of loving our country is very much to the point.

Consciously of unconsciously our citizens are grouping themselves around the only two possible ultimate answers to the questions vexing our country. The first answer is that the essence of Americanism is revolution; the second answer is that the essence of Americanism consists in the recognition of the sacredness of human personality.

First let us consider the revolutionary theory. The Communists, in their attempt to justify another revolution, are rewriting American history to suit the dialectics of Marx and Lenin. Their argument is this: America began with a revolution; the real descendants then of our national forefathers are those who believe in revolution; but the Communists believe in revolutionary theory and practice; therefore they are the true Americans.

In support of this thesis the General Secretary of the Communist Party in the United States, writes in his work *What is Communism*: "The revolutionary tradition is the heart of Americanism.... We Communists claim the revolutionary traditions of Americanism. We are the only ones who consciously continue those traditions and apply them to the problems of today. *We are the Americans and Communism is the Americanism of the 20th Century....* Our American giants of 1776 were the 'international incendiaries' of their day. They inspired revolutions throughout the world."[87] "The reactionaries will rise up against us; they will denounce us as Reds, and revolutionists. Of this we need not be afraid. Revolution is the essence of the American tradition."[88]

Before passing on to the opposing theory concerning the essence of Americanism, it might be well to investigate the value of the Communist theory. Is it logical? There probably is no one who uses even one of his intellectual lobes, who cannot see the fallacy of the argument. First of all to argue that because the Communists believe in revolution, therefore they are the heirs of the Revolutionary War, is just as stupid as to say that every American who wears a red coat is a descendant of an English soldier. Furthermore, since when does the Revolutionary War give a man the right to be revolutionary? Does it give you and me the right to drive through red traffic lights, even though they are of the Communist color? And why should revolution be the unique right of the Communists? Why should it not be the right of everyone, for that is the meaning of revolution.

---

[87] Earl Browder, "Who Are the Americans", *What Is Communism?* (New York: Workers Library Publications, 1936), 19–21.

[88] Earl Browder, *Lincoln and the Communists* (New York: Workers Library Publications, 1936), 13.

Then every fool is entitled to be revolutionary who would turn our country into a great free-for-all.

It is no more true to say that "Communism is 20th century Americanism," for America never contemplated in its Constitution a Dictator whether he be Bolshevik or Fascist. If "Communism is 20th Century Americanism" why does the Communist Party of the United States remain affiliated with Communist International of Moscow? Why does it agree not to hold a Congress in the United States without the permission of the Communist Executive Committee of Moscow, according to Article 34 of its Constitution with Moscow? Why does it allow its candidate for President of the United States to become a member of the Moscow Presidium? Oh! How they would howl if any other candidate for President of the United States were even just an honorary member of the Nazis. Why did the Communist Party of the United States send delegates to the last Moscow Congress? Why did the official organ of the Communist International of Moscow say the book of the Secretary of the Communist Party in the United States was in complete accord with the new tactics of the Communist International of Moscow? Why did the leaders of the Communist Party in the United States on July 27th and 28th, 1935, stand on their feet in Moscow and cheer "Stalin, the leader of the world revolution"? If an alliance with Moscow is 20th century Americanism; if revolution, violence, "ruthless suppression of minorities", "confiscation", "purging of the old dross of society", is 20th century Americanism, then how does America differ from Moscow? If America believed that "Communism were 20th century Americanism" our government would never have signed an agreement with Russia as it did in 1931, specifying that a commercial treaty did not give them the right to carry on the propaganda of the revolutionary Third International in this country. Russia has broken this agreement a thousand times over, and the reason we have done nothing about it is that American common sense has refused and will refuse to follow any system which in one day can execute seven generals of the army, three newspaper editors, two members of the cabinet, and all the governors of its states. If they insist on appealing to the American Revolution we would remind them that it was a political revolution against a government across the sea, and not a civil war and class struggle against one another. In any case, what was the end and purpose of the Revolutionary War? It was to keep a foreign power out of America. The real heirs of the American Revolution are therefore not the Communists, but those who in 1938 attempt to keep another foreign power out of America, whether it be Fascist or Communist.

Now for an important warning about insidious propaganda:

1) Do not be fooled by Communist propaganda that Communism is democracy. Democracy means the right of minorities to dissent, but Communism permits neither minorities nor dissent. Furthermore, democracy believes in parliamentary reform; Communism believes in revolution. Democracy believes in the right of people to choose a leader; Communism believes in the right of a Dictator to "choose" himself by purging his opposition. Communism calls itself a democracy to fool us, and here is the proof: American Communists were told by Moscow to talk democracy to us, but not to believe in it. Dimitrov told the Americans, quoting Lenin, that "It would be a fundamental mistake to suppose that the struggle for democracy can divert the proletariat from the Social revolution, or obscure or overshadow it".[89] And Manuilsky told them that the United Front tactics of talking democracy did not mean that Communism had capitulated to democracy, and if they believed it did they were

---

[89] *Working Class Unity: Bulwark Against Fascism*, 129.

"downright scoundrels" and "hopeless idiots".[90] If Communism is democracy then Stalin loves Trotsky.

2) Never defend America, politically against Communism without at the same time defending it against Nazism and Fascism, for the simple reason that dictatorship and democracy do not go together. Beware of any organization for peace, for youth, for democracy, e.g. "The American League for Peace and Democracy", which condemns one without the other. If, for example, you find an organization condemning Fascism or Nazism without condemning Communism, you may be sure that it is only a question of the pot calling the kettle black. As an American you must be opposed to all Dictators, Fascist, Nazi, or Communist. The Communist trick is to accuse all who are opposed to Communism of being Fascists. This is not true. Because I dislike Russian caviar it does not follow that I am mad about spaghetti or wiener-schnitzel. The tactics of Communism in relation to Fascism are very much like those of the prize fighter who whispered to his opponent in a clinch that his shoe-string was untied, whereupon the boxer let down his guard to tie his show and was cracked into oblivion. So too Communism says, "Look out for Fascism"—and as we become excited about it, Communism worms its way in for the kill. The proper American attitude is to keep both out of America.

Now, how to do that? The best way to keep Fascism out of American life is to keep out Communism. The reason is simple. Historically, Fascism has arisen as a reaction against Communism, as a counter-irritant to Communism. It arose that way in Italy and Germany and in other countries. It did not arise as a separate and independent movement, but as an exaggerated response to the danger of violent revolution.

---

[90] *The Work of the Seventh Congress*, 58–59.

That is why in Europe every forward growth of Communism has produced a military dictatorship. Fascism is not first, but Communism. Fascism is the reaction against Communism. If then you want to keep Fascism out of America, the best thing to do is to keep out Communism. The danger of both grows proportionately, just as jails grow proportionately with criminals. It is not very likely that Communism will ever gain a foothold in America, simply because of the innate common sense of the American people. But we must avoid being stampeded by pressure groups, either Fascist or Communist. If Communism grows, the American people may be stampeded into a Fascist reaction; and if the Fascist danger is exaggerated, we may be stampeded into a Communist reaction. The best thing for us to do is to keep our heads and do our thinking according to American principles and not swallow sugarcoated propaganda. In other words, if you do not want to smell up your closets with Fascist mothballs, then keep out the Communist moths; for the moths come first, then the mothballs. If you do not want your parlor cluttered up with rat-traps, then keep out the rats; if you do not want an anti-Communist dictator then do not want a Communist dictator; if you do not want a Hitler in America, then don't let the Communists talk you into a Stalin.

The essence of Americanism is not revolution but the recognition of the sacredness of human personality and the inherent inalienable rights which every man possesses independently of the State. That is why, when our country began, our Founding Fathers were most anxious to find some basis for human rights, some foundation for human liberties, some guarantee of human personality which would be above the encroachment of tyranny and abuse. But where do we find the basis for the right of a man to be his own master, captain of his own soul, free in his right to pursue his ultimate end with a free conscience? Where do we root and ground the right to own property as the extension of personality? Where can we find the rock of all liberties which would be strong enough to withstand governments and powers and states which would absorb them as the monarchies did then, and as certain dictatorships do now?

For such a foundation the Fathers looked first to England. There the theory was advanced that our liberties and rights are rooted in Parliament. This theory they rejected on the ground that if Parliament gives rights and liberties, then the Parliament can take them away.

Next they looked to France, where it was held that the liberties and rights of man are rooted in the will of the majority. The Fathers equally rejected this on the ground that if the rights of man are the gift of the majority, then the majority can take away the rights of the minority. Where do we find the source of the liberties and the rights of man? On what stable foundations are they to be reared? What is their source?

The answer they gave was the right one. They sought the foundations of man's rights and liberties in something so sacred and so inalienable that no State, no Parliament, no Dictator, no human power could ever take them away, and so they rooted them in God. Hence our Declaration of Independence reads: "... All men ... are endowed by their Creator with certain unalienable Rights ... among these are Life, Liberty, and the pursuit of Happiness." Note that the word used is "unalienable"; that means that these rights belong to the sacredness of human personality and are not the gift of the State or the Dictator, whether Fascist, Nazi, or Communist.

In other words, man's right to own private property, man's right to educate his own family, man's right to adore God according to the dictates of his conscience, come not from the Constitution, the Government, Parliament, or the will of the majority, but from God. Therefore no power on earth may take them away. This is the essence of Americanism. Now, if the essence of Americanism is the sacredness of human personality as created by God, who is doing most to preserve that Americanism? The schools that never mention His name? The universities and colleges that dissolve the Deity into the latest ultimate of physics and biology? The professors who adjust their ethics to suit unethical lives?

The answer obviously is, that the forces that are building constructive Americanism are those that take practical cognizance of the existence of God. It is the non-religious schools which are out of the tradition of Americanism; they are on the defensive. In the beginning of our national life practically all of our schools and colleges were religious schools. It was assumed by our Constitution and by its spirit that they would be religious. The reason was obvious. If human dignity and liberty come from God, then it follows that loss of faith in Him means loss of faith in those liberties which derive from Him. If we wish to have the light we must keep the sun; if we wish to keep our forests we must keep our trees; if we wish to keep our perfumes we must keep our flowers—and if we wish to keep our rights then we must keep our God.

We Catholics are taking religion so seriously in reference to our country that rather than see God perish out of our national life we conduct 7,929 elementary schools and 1,945 high schools, employing 58,903 and 16,784 teachers respectively. These schools represent an investment of about 750 million dollars for elementary schools and about 575 million dollars for high schools. To keep the system going we spend approximately 58 million dollars a year on elementary schools and approximately ten million dollars a year on high schools; and figuring on the basis of public school costs, we save the taxpayers of the country an immediate one billion dollar building program and, for maintenance, about $139,600,000 every year. Every cent of this money comes out of the pockets of Catholics, and why? Because we believe that the 2,102,889 children in Catholic elementary schools and 284,736 in Catholic high schools have a right to know the truth which makes them free. In other words, we take very seriously the Declaration of Independence which derives the rights of man from God.

In conclusion, true Americanism is the belief in the freedom of man as a divine derivative. For that reason if we wish to keep pure Americanism we must keep our religion. To this is to be added the important fact that dictatorships, such as the Communist, regard man only as a stomach to be fed by the State, or as a tool to amass wealth for the State. Put men on that level and they need no religion, any more than animals need religion, or a monkey wrench needs liturgy. But to put them on that level is to depersonalize and mechanize them down to the very core of their being. A democracy needs religion, for it assumes that man has not only a stomach but also a soul which is the seat of his rights; and since that soul must be fed as well as the body, he must have religion.

Democracy has to rely not on force, but on freedom and liberty. But freedom and liberty are inseparable from responsibility, and responsibility is inseparable from conscience, and conscience is inseparable from religion.

It is our solemn duty as Catholics, therefore, to be conscious of our duty to America, and to preserve its freedom by preserving its faith in God against that group which would identify revolution with Americanism. We must protest that there are stars in our flag, not a hammer and sickle, to remind us that the destiny of human life is beyond the implements of daily toil—beyond the stars and the "hid battlements of eternity",[91] with God. The Communists want the flag red. We are willing to have a little red in it, but we want some white and blue in it too. Then the red will not stand for revolution but for sacrifice, and above all else a sacrifice inspired by the death of him Who on Calvary proved the greatest love of all. Then the blue in it will remind us that we must be loyal to America, never daring to subvert it even under the gentle name of "United Front". Then the white in it will remind us that we must keep it pure and un-Moscowized. But as we talk about patriotism, it might be well to remind ourselves that in crisis like this even devotion to the Stars and Stripes is not enough to save us. We must look beyond them to other stars and stripes, namely the stars and stripes of Christ, by whose stars we are illumined by whose stripes we are healed.

---

[91] Francis Thompson, *The Hound of Heaven* (Maine: Thomas B. Mosher, 1908).

CHARITY

Address delivered on February 27, 1938

The Holy Father offers something "still more important as a remedy for [Communism], or certainly more directly calculated to cure it, [namely] the precept of charity". "We have in mind," he writes, "that Christian charity, 'patient and kind', which avoids all semblance of demeaning paternalism, and all ostentation; that charity which from the very beginning of Christianity won to Christ the poorest of the poor, the slaves".[92] The more the workingman and the poor realize what the spirit of love animated by the virtue of Christ is doing for them, the more readily will they abandon the false persuasion that Christianity has lost its efficacy and that the Church stands on the side of the exploiters of their labor.

The Church is here addressing her own children, and not alone those who have, but those who have not, for the precept of charity applies to both the rich and the poor. If the rich hate the poor and the poor hate the rich it is because both have offended against charity, the rich by being too selfish and the poor by being too envious. The rich who exploit the poor and the poor who would violently dispossess the rich are extremes equally wrong and therefore equally to be condemned. To both the precept of charity must be preached.

---

[92] *Divini Redemptoris*, no. 46.

I. TO THE RICH:

The precept of charity teaches the rich that they are but stewards of wealth and that they have the necessity of being detached from their wealth out of love for the poor.

(a) As regards the stewardship of wealth the Church says: "The rich should ... [consider] themselves only a stewards of their earthly goods, [and be] mindful of the account they must render of them to their Lord and Master, and value them as precious means that God has put into their hands for doing good; let them not fail, besides, to distribute of their abundance to the poor, according to the evangelical precept."[93]

The stewardship of wealth means that wealth is not a possession, but a trust. On the principle of stewardship wealth is something we hold from God, and for which we must render an account; it is nothing wholly personal like an heirloom, but something functional like a university endowment; it must be used for good purposes. Wealth requires justification, and it may be justified on benevolent grounds or aesthetic grounds. Of its benevolent use Our Lord spoke when He said to the rich young man: "Yet one thing is wanting to thee: sell all whatever thou hast, and give to the poor, and thou shalt have treasure in heaven: and come, follow me."[94] Of the aesthetic use of wealth, Our Lord spoke the day He was anointed by the precious ointment of a converted sinner, for which she received the promise that her good deed would be recorded to the end of time. In this day there are those who seeing wealth given to the adornment of God's altar, condemn the Church for accepting it, as Judas on that day seeing ointment poured on the feet of the Savior, might have asked: "Why all this waste?"

---

[93] *Ibid.*, no. 44.

[94] Luke 18:22.

The rich must justify their right on wealth; they may not assume that the first claim on their money is their own comfort, or that they need give no alms until all their imaginable comforts are satisfied, or that their possessions must determine their station in life rather than their station in life determine the use of their possessions.

(b) The right of a rich man to his wealth is secondary to the starving man's right to the satisfaction of his human needs. The rich man therefore must detach himself from his wealth out of charity for the sake of the poor, and if the need of the poor is acute, the obligation to do so becomes one of strict justice. But even charity calls for a sharing of abundance with the needy, for the superfluities of the rich are the necessities of the poor. As St. Augustine put it: "The burden of the poor is their not having what they absolutely need; the burden of the rich is their having what they do not absolutely need." Scripture records no other reason why Dives lost his soul than because he dined sumptuously each day, was clothed in fine linen, and ignored Lazarus the beggar at his door. He failed to see that the crumbs from his table which were superfluities to him were necessities to Lazarus. In the eyes of the world Dives must have been a great man, because he was rich; in the eyes of God Dives was a lost soul, an eternal failure, because he ignored the poor.

This Gospel story points to a theory and practice of life which is not in harmony with that which is practiced by a great percentage of our population, but which, if it were put into practice, would revolutionize society in a day. Many rich Christians are good-natured, benevolent, cultivated, and have fine natural virtues, but too few give to the poor because they fail to see Our Lord walking in their worn shoes. We must not see virtue in the poor before we help them, for the demand is that *virtue* be in us, and if we refuse to give, it is we who are

lacking virtue. "Give to everyone that asketh thee."[95] Neither must
we consider whether the poor are our enemies or our friends,
for Christ is in their poverty and not in their enmity. That is
why He said: "And if you do good to them who do good to you,
what thanks are to you? For sinners also do this.... But love ye
your enemies: do good, and lend, hoping for nothing thereby:
and your reward shall be great, and you shall be the sons of
the Highest; for he is kind to the unthankful, and to the evil."[96]

Because the gloved hand reaches out for the gift, we nevertheless know we are giving it to the person; in like manner, the
dirty hand of the poor man is the glove of the Person of Christ.
All ye who have, remember! He is walking to your doors on the
feet of the hungry; He is asking you for a drink through the
parched tongues of the sick; He is bumping into you at your
street corners in the person of a beggar; He is looking in through
your windows as a Lazarus as you dine as a Dives; His mother
is knocking at your portals as Mary did at Bethlehem, asking
just for an inn where the Savior might be born. If Bethlehem
only knew! If we only suspected! The next time you refuse the
poor, ask yourself this question: "What if that man be Christ?"

II. TO THE POOR

Now for a word about the poor. Charity is just as binding upon
them as on the rich, but in a different way. The law of Charity
warns the rich against being selfish; and it warns the poor against
being envious. "The poor too, in their turn, while engaged,
according to the laws of charity and justice, in acquiring the
necessities of life and also in bettering their condition, should

---

[95] Luke 6:30.

[96] Luke 6:33,35.

always remain "poor in spirit", and hold spiritual goods in higher esteem than earthly property and pleasures."[97]

Note that the Church does not say the poor must remain poor; rather she says the poor ought to "better their condition", but at the same time they must remain "poor in spirit". There is a world of difference between the poor and the poor in spirit. The poor are generally the destitute. The poor in spirit may be the rich providing they are detached from their wealth. The Church wants no one to be poor in the sense of miserable—not even those who take the vow of poverty. That vow does not oblige a priest or a nun to be hungry all through life, and to be denied a bed and shelter; rather it obliges him or her to be content with the necessities of life and not to seek more. These poor in spirit who give up everything, by a peculiar paradox, possess everything, for there is nothing they desire. No man can have the whole world, but he can renounce the whole world. He cannot possess it, but he can dispossess it; it is not his to own, but it is his to disown; he can not draw the whole world into his hands, but he can wash his hands of it; there being nothing more he wants, he is therefore the richest man in the world. This is the ideal poverty implied by the vow of poverty, it does want everyone to be "poor in spirit". The poor in our country who would violently dispossess the rich, who join the Communists because of the promise to "overthrow capitalism by force" and to "liquidate" all who own, and who sow seeds of hatred against their fellowman, are not the Gospel poor. Their only regret is that they cannot be rich; their souls are just as avaricious as the souls of the selfish rich. They are the involuntary poor, the poor who crave to be rich; the enemies of Capitalists because they want to be Capitalists themselves. They are scandalized at

---

[97] *Divini Redemptoris*, no. 45.

the wealth of others but only after they are tempted by the lust for its possession. That is why every Communist is at heart a Capitalist without any cash in his pockets. He talks more about his hatred of the rich than his love of the poor; more about the evils of the present system than the remedies he has to offer. This group with hatred of classes is just as much a menace to our civilization as the rich who exploit the poor. The verdict of history is against them; those envious poor who crushed the rich never did anything for the poor man with all their confiscated wealth; they merely transferred individual selfishness into collective selfishness. They therefore have no right to condemn the rich; they have never earned the right. No man has a right to condemn the rich until, like our Blessed Lord, he has proved he is free from the passion of wealth.

Charity also enjoins upon the poor a recognition that no human system can ever offer perfect peace and happiness, otherwise earth would be heaven, and this life would not be novitiate for the next. "Let [the poor] remember that the world will never be able to rid itself of misery, sorrow and tribulation, which are the portion even of those who seem most prosperous. Patience, therefore, is the need of all, that Christian patience which comforts the heart with the divine assurance of eternal happiness".[98]

Lenin ridicules this Christian doctrine by saying that religion asks us "to bear misfortunes uncomplainingly. It thus provides a justification for exploitation as if it were a cheap ticket to Heaven". In other words, it preaches a resignation which is passivity because "it teaches those who toil in poverty to be resigned and patient in this world and consoles them with the hope of a reward in heaven".

---

[98] *Divini Redemptoris*, no. 45.

It simply is not true that religion preaches passivity to unjust conditions. If it did, Leo XIII and Pius XI would never have written their encyclicals in defense of the working man, in which the former states: "It is [the duty of the State] to promote in the highest degree the interests of the poor.... [It is the desire of the Church] that the poor ... should rise above poverty and wretchedness, and should better their condition in [this] life; and for this it strives."[99] As a matter of fact there has never been written such a strong protest against economic injustices as in these encyclical letters.

Furthermore, the resignation which religion preaches is not passive submission to economic injustice as Communism contends. Resignation means accepting our lot while working to better conditions by an intelligent understanding of the nature of things. A mother, for example, is resigned to the pettiness and helplessness of her new born babe; a farmer is resigned to the slow maturing of the seed he sows in the springtime—because both take into account the *nature* of things. But because the mother is resigned to infancy, or because the farmer is resigned to the seasons, it does not follow that they are passive or inactive, or that the mother does not nourish her babe, or the farmer till his crops. As a matter of fact, they both work intelligently to draw out the perfection of the things committed to their care.

So it is with religion. Religion is resigned to the nature of the world and the nature of man. It knows very well that man is prone to evil, that some selfishness will remain under any economic system, and that no paradise can be built here below. But because religion is resigned to these practical limitations, religion does not refuse to better conditions by infusing virtue into the hearts and souls of men, to the end of making a world

---

[99] *Rerum Novarum*, nos. 26, 23.

where the good can live among the bad, where the rich can live without exploiting the poor, the poor can live without being violently destructive of all wealth, and where the majority can live in a state this side of heroism and martyrdom. Communism, however, refuses to accept the nature of things and thinks it can change them by violence and confiscation. But it is just as foolish to think that by a revolution one can alter the nature of man, as it is to believe that you can alter the nature of a baby by putting a bomb under its cradle, blowing it up and expecting it to come down a full grown Bolshevik. In fact it is just as foolish to try to build a perfect paradise here below by revolution, as it is to try to dynamite triangles into four-sided figures. There are certain things to which we must be resigned and the nature of man is one It is simply because Russia has refused to take account of this one fact that it has failed. All its failures are failures incidental to human nature. Since it failed to be resigned to that, it must be resigned to failure.

The spirit of Charity will do much, not only to weaken the vindictiveness of those who attack the unfulfilled duties of the rich, but it will also do much to make us live in peace and concord with our fellowman. *The Communist solution is to make the poor hate the rich; the Christian solution is to make the rich love the poor.* The reason why the Communists make the poor hate the rich is to set society in such a state of chaos that they can establish their dictatorship of the proletariat; the reason why Christians want to make the rich love the poor is that all may enjoy the heritages and benefits of civilization, and in order that the poor man, relieved from the worry of eking out an insecure livelihood, may be free enough to save his soul.

The Communists speak only of the proletarian; the Christian speaks of the poor. The proletarian is the worker who can be used to overthrow existing society and set up a Soviet regime; the poor is everyman—he may even be the Communist who hates you. The proletariat is the abstract—the mass, the collectivity, the mob that can be thrown into hysteria by this "vanguard and leader", as the Communist Party calls itself; the poor is the concrete—the person, the unemployed barber, the sick minister without a pulpit, the Jewish father who has just lost his sole supporting son. The proletariat is a class; the poor is every man, friend and enemy. The proletarian wants not only his own goods but those of his neighbor; the poor wants to have sufficient of his own goods and believes his neighbor should have the same. The Communist wants to make the proletarian hate his employers as a thief; the Christian wants to make the employer practice a moral virtue and give to every man his due. The Communist feeds the proletariat to make more wealth for the state; the Christian feeds the poor to leave their souls free to think about something other than a sickle and a hammer.

America is broader and bigger than the proletarian class; it has poor in it who are not workers and who cannot work. Hence it needs something more than Communism: it needs Charity. Hatred and selfishness will not save society because they are essentially destructive; only a spirit of Charity poured out lavishly from the throne of Christ can so order it, that the rich will anticipate the needs of the poor, and the poor will be grateful to the rich.

Not to that narrow group called the proletariat have we been sent, but to the poor which includes the proletariat as the animal kingdom includes the horse. The Church recruited her strength from them in the beginning and it is from them again that she will draw her new strength. As Catholics we must be conscious of our duty to them as never before, and it is our solemn duty to go down to the masses and build up just as strong and vigorous a body of noble men and women dedicated to peace, to their God, and to their country, as the Communists would build up a revolutionary proletariat. The banner of "lovers of the poor" shall not be taken from our hands by those who shriek hatred of the rich. We are born of the Poor Man of Galilee and lovers of the poor we must be, even though it means the sacrifice of our comfort and the touch of Calvary's Cross. Share with them your wealth, for on that condition you are admitted to the Church of the poor; give even to the poor who hate you, as Christ forgave His enemies, and as the Holy Father appointed a commission to aid in feeding the starving Russians. And be not deceived! Communism is the philosophy of the wealthy; it is the studied system of making the proletariat rich by confiscation. The poor therefore are ours, and ours they will be even unto the end of time.

⚖️ UNJUST SUFFERING

(The First Word from the Cross)

Address delivered on March 6, 1938

The world is full of those who suffer unjustly and who through no fault of their own bear the "slings and arrows of outrageous fortune". What should be their attitude to those who speak untruly of them, who malign their good names, who steal their reputations, and who sneer at their acts of kindness?

The answer is to be found in the first word from the Cross: *forgive*. If there was ever anyone who had a right to protest against injustice, it was He Who is Divine Justice; if ever there was anyone who was entitled to reproach those who dug his hands and feet with steel, it was Our Lord on the Cross. And yet at that very moment when a tree turns against Him and becomes a cross, when iron turns against Him and becomes nails, when roses turn against Him and become thorns, when men turn against Him and become executioners, He lets fall from His lips for the first time in the history of the world a prayer for enemies: "Father, forgive them, for they know not what they do."[100]

Dwell for a moment on what He did not say. He did not say: "I am innocent", and yet who else could have better claimed innocence? Many times before this Good Friday and many times

---

[100] Luke 23:34.

since, men have been sent to a cross, a guillotine, or a scaffold, for a crime they never committed; but not one of them has ever failed to cry: "I am innocent."

But Our Lord made no such protest, for it would have been to have falsely assumed that man is the Judge of God. Now if Our Lord, Who was Innocence, refrained from asserting His Innocence, then we who are not without sin should not forever be crying our innocence. To do this is wrongly to admit that man, and not God, is our Judge. Our souls are to be judged not before the tribunal of men, but before the throne of the God of love; and He "who sees in secret will reward in secret."[101] Our eternal salvation does not depend on how the world judges us, but on how God judges us. It matters little if our fellow citizens condemn us even when we are right, for Truth always finds its contradictors; that is why Truth is now nailed to a Cross. What does matter is that we be found right in God's judgment, for in that our eternal happiness depends. There is every chance in the world that the two judgments will differ, for man sees only the face, but God reads the heart. We can fool men, but we cannot fool God.

There was another thing Our Blessed Lord did not say to the representatives of Caesar and the Temple who sent Him to the Cross, namely, "You are unjust". The Father gave all judgment unto Him and yet He does not judge them and say: "You will suffer for this." He knew, being God as well as man, that while there is life there is hope, and His patient suffering before death might purchase the souls of many who now condemn. Why judge them before the time for judgment? Longinus of the Roman army and Joseph of the Sanhedrin would come to His saving embrace and forgiveness even before He was taken

---

[101] Matt. 6:6.

down from the Cross. The sinner of this hour might be the saint of the next. One reason for a long life is penance. Time is given us not just to accumulate that which we cannot take with us, but to discharge ourselves of those faults and sins which we ought not take with us. That is why in the parable of the fig tree which had not borne fruit for three years and which the owner wished to cut down because it "cumbereth the ground", the dresser of the vineyard said: "Let it alone this year also, until I dig about it, and dung it. And if happily it bear fruit."[102] So the Lord is with the wicked. He gives them another month, another year of life that they may dig their soul with penance and dung it with mortification, and happily save their souls. If the Lord did not judge His executioners before the hour of their judgment, why should we, who really know nothing about them anyway, judge them even when they do us wrong? While they live, may not our refraining from judgment be the very means of their conversion? In any case, judgment has not been given to us, and the world may be thankful that it has not, for God is a more merciful judge than man. "Judge not that you may not be judged."[103]

What Our Lord did say on the Cross was *forgive*. Forgive your Pilates, who are too weak to defend your justice; forgive your Herods, who are too sensual to perceive your spirituality; forgive your Judases, who think worth is to be measured in terms of silver. "Forgive them—for they know not what they do." In that sentence is packed the united love of Father and Son, whereby the holy love of God met the sin of man, and remained innocent. This first word of forgiveness is the strongest evidence of Our Lord's absolute sinlessness. The rest of us at our death

---

[102] Luke 13:6-9.

[103] Matt. 7:1.

must witness the great parade of our sins, and the sight of them
is so awful that we dare not go before God without a prayer for
pardon. Yet Jesus, on dying, craved no forgiveness, for He had
no sin. The forgiveness He asked was for those who accused
Him of sin. And the reason He asked for pardon was because
"they know not what they do". He is God as well as man, which
means He knows all the secrets of every human heart. Because
He knows all, He can find an excuse: "they know not what they
do." But we know so little of our enemies' hearts and so little
of the circumstances of their acts and the good faith mingled
with their evil deeds, that any judgment we make concerning
them is apt to be wrong.

In order to judge others we must be inside of them and
outside of them, but only God can do this. Our neighbors are
just as impenetrable to us as we are to them. Judgment on our
part, then, would be wrong, for to judge without a mandate is
unjust. Our Lord alone has a mandate to judge; we have not. If
possessing that mandate, and knowing all, He still found reason
to forgive, then we who have no jurisdiction and who cannot
possibly with our puny minds know our neighbors' hearts, have
only one thing left to do, and that is, to pray: "Father, forgive ...
for they know not what they do."

Our Lord used the word, *forgive*, because He was innocent
and knew all, but we must use it for other reasons. First, because
we have been forgiven greater sins by God. Secondly, because
only by forgiving can hate be banished from the world. And
thirdly, because our own pardon is conditioned on the pardon
we extend to others.

Firstly, we must forgive others because God has forgiven us.
There is no injustice any human being has ever committed against
us which is comparable to the injustice we commit against God
by our sins. It is this idea Our Lord suggests in the parable of

the unmerciful servant who was forgiven a debt of ten thousand talents by his master, and immediately afterwards went out and choked a fellow-servant who owed him only a hundred pence.[104] The debt which the master forgave the servant was 1,250,000 times greater than the debt owed by the fellow-servant. In this great disproportion is revealed how much greater are man's sins against God than are the sins of our enemies, because we have been forgiven the greater sin of treating God as an enemy. And if we do not forgive the sins of our enemies, it is very likely because we have never cast up our accounts with God. Herein is to be found the secret of so much of the violence and bitterness of some men in our modern world; they refuse to think of themselves as ever having offended God and therefore never think of themselves as needing pardon. They think they need no pardon, hence no one else should ever have it. The man who knows not his own guilt before God is apt to be most unforgiving to others, as David at the time of his worst sin.[105]

Our condemnation is often the alibi for our own weakness: we cover up our own nakedness with the mantle of criticism; we see the mote in our brother's eye, but never the beam in our own. We carry all our neighbor's faults on a rack in front of us, and all our own on a rack behind us. The cruelest master is the man who never learned to obey, and the severest judge is the man who never examines his own conscience. The man who is conscious of his need of absolution is the one who is most likely to be indulgent to others, such as Paul who, writing to Titus, finds a reason for being merciful to men: "For we ourselves also were some time unwise, incredulous, erring, slaves to divers desires and pleasures, living in malice and envy, hateful, and

---

[104] Matt. 18:21-35.

[105] 2 Kgs. 12:5.

hating one another".[106] It is the forgetfulness of its own sins which makes modern hate so deep and bitter. Men throttle their neighbor for a penny because they forget God forgave them a debt of ten thousand talents. Let them only think of how good God has been to them, and they will begin to be good to others.

A second reason for forgiving those who make us suffer unjustly is that if we do not forgive, hate will multiply until the whole world is hateful. Hate is extremely fertile; it reproduces itself with amazing rapidity. Communism knows hate can disrupt society more quickly than armies, that is why it never speaks of charity. That too is why it sows hatred in Labor against Capital; hatred in atheists against religion; hatred in themselves against all who oppose them. How can all this hatred be stopped when one man is slapping another on the cheek? There is only one way, and that is by turning the other cheek, which means: "I forgive; I refuse to hate you. If I hate you, I will add my quota to the sum-total of hate. This I refuse to do. I will kill your hate, I will drive it from the earth. I will love you."

That was the way Stephen conquered the hate of those who killed him; namely, by praying: "LORD, lay not this sin to their charge."[107] He was practically repeating the first word from the Cross. And that prayer of forgiveness won over the heart of a young man named Saul who stood nearby, holding the garments of those who stoned him, and "consenting to his death". If Stephen had cursed Saul, Saul might never have become St. Paul. What a loss that would have been! But hate lost the day because Stephen forgave.

In our day love is still winning victories over hate. When Father (Miguel) Pro of Mexico a few years ago was shot by the

---

[106] Titus 3:3.

[107] Acts 7:59.

Mexican revolutionists, he turned to them and said: "I forgive you; kneel and I will give you my blessing." And every soldier in the firing line fell on his knees for the blessing. It was a beautiful spectacle indeed to see a man forgiving those who are about to kill him! Only the Captain refused to kneel, and it was he who did what to Father Pro was an act of great kindness—ushered him, by a blow through the heart, into the company of Stephen, a martyr of the Church of God.

Within the past year when the Reds of Spain were slaughtering hundreds of priests, one of them was lined up before the firing squad with his arms tightly bound by ropes. Facing the firing squad, he said: "Untie these ropes and let me give you my blessing before I die." The Communists untied the ropes, but they cut off his hands. Then sarcastically they said: "All right, see if you can give us your blessing now." And the priest raised the stumps of his arms as crimson rags and with blood dripping from them like beads forming on the earth the red rosary of redemption, he moved them about in the form of a cross. Thus hate was defeated for he refused to nourish it. Hate died as he forgave and the world has been better for it.

Finally, we must forgive others, for on no other condition will our own sins be forgiven. In fact, it is almost a moral impossibility for God to forgive us unless we in turn forgive. Has He not said: "Blessed are the merciful: for they shall obtain mercy",[108] "Forgive, and you shall be forgiven. Give, and it shall be given unto you.... For with the same measure that you shall mete withal, it shall be measured to you again."[109] The law is inescapable. Unless we throw something up, it will not come down; unless we sow, we shall not reap; unless we show mercy

---

[108] Matt. 5:7.

[109] Luke 6:37-38.

to our fellowmen, God will revoke His mercy toward us. As in the parable the master canceled the forgiveness of the servant because he refused to show a smaller mercy to his fellowman, "so also shall my heavenly Father do to you, if you forgive not every one his brother from your hearts".[110]

If a box is filled with salt it cannot be filled with sand, and if our hearts are filled with hatred of our neighbor how can God fill them with His love? It is just as simple as that. There can be and there will be no mercy toward others unless we ourselves are merciful. The real test of the Christian then is not how much he loves his friends, but how much he loves his enemies. The divine command is clear: "Love your enemies: do good to them that hate you: and pray for them that persecute and calumniate you: that you may be the children of your Father who is in heaven, who maketh his sun to rise upon the good, and bad, and raineth upon the just and the unjust. For if you love them that love you, what reward shall you have? Do not even the publicans this? And if you salute your brethren only, what do you more? Do not also the heathens this?"[111]

Forgive, then! Forgive even seventy times seven! Soften the pillow of death by forgiving your enemies their little sins against you, that you may be forgiven your great sins against God. Forgive those who injure you, that you may be forgiven your offenses. Our world is so full of hate! The race of the clenched fists is multiplying like the race of Cain. The struggle for existence has become existence for struggle. There are even those who talk about peace only because they want the world to wait until they are strong enough for war.

---

[110] Matt. 18:35.

[111] Matt. 5:44-47.

Dear Lord, what can we, Thy followers, do to bring peace to the world? How can we stop brother rising up against brother and class against class, blurring the very sky with their cross-covered Golgathas? Thy First Word on the Cross gives the answer: We must see in the body of every man who hates, a soul that was made to love. If we are too easily offended by their hate, it is because we have forgotten either the destiny of their souls or our own who trespass against us. Forgive us for ever having been offended. Then we, like Thee, may find among our executioners another Longinus, who had forgotten there was love in a heart until we opened it with a lance.

PAIN

(The Second Word from the Cross)

Address delivered on March 13, 1938

The *First Word* tells us what should be our attitude toward unjust suffering, but the *Second Word* tells us what should be our attitude towards pain. There are two ways of looking at it; one is to see it without purpose, the other to see it with purpose. The first view regards pain as something opaque, like a stone wall; the other view regards it as something transparent, like a window pane. The way we will react to it depends entirely upon our philosophy of life. As the poet has put it:

Two men looked out through their prison bars;
The one saw mud, the other stars.

In like manner, there are those who, looking upon a rose, would say: "Isn't it a pity that roses have thorns?", while others would say, "Isn't it consoling that thorns have roses?" These two attributes are manifested in the two thieves crucified on either side of Our Blessed Lord. The thief on the right is the model for those for whom pain has a meaning.

Consider first the thief on the left. He suffered just as much as the thief on the right, but he began and ended his crucifixion with a curse. Never for a moment did he correlate his sufferings with the Man on the central cross. Our Lord's prayer of forgiveness, and His patient bearing, meant no more to that thief than the flight of a bird. He saw no more purpose in his pain than a fly sees purpose in the window pane that floods man's habitation with God's warmth and sunlight. Because he could not assimilate his pain and make it turn to the nourishment of his soul, pain turned against him as a foreign substance taken into the stomach turns against it and infects and poisons the whole system. That is why he became bitter, why his mouth became like a crater of hate, and why he cursed the very Lord Who could have shepherded him into peace and paradise.

The world today is full of those who, like the thief on the left, see no meaning in pain. Knowing nothing of Redemption they are unable to fit pain into a pattern; it becomes just an odd patch on the crazy quilt of life. Life becomes so wholly unpredictable for them that "a troubled manhood follows their baffled youth".[112] Never having thought of God as anything more than a name, they are now unable to fit the stark realities of life into His Divine Plan. That is why so many who cease to believe in God become cynics, killing not only themselves but, in a certain sense, even the beauties of flowers and the faces of children for whom they refuse to live.

The lesson is clear: Pain of itself does not make us better; it is very apt to make us worse. No man was ever better simply because he had an earache. Unspiritualized suffering does not improve man; it degenerates him. The thief at the left is no better for his crucifixion: it sears him, burns him, and tarnishes his soul. Refusing to think of pain as related to anything else, he ends by thinking only of himself and who would take him down from the cross. So it is with those who have lost their faith in God. To them Our Lord on a cross is only an event in the

---

[112] George Gordon Byron, *The Complete Works of Lord Byron* (Paris: Baudry's European Library, 1857).

history of the Roman empire. He is not a message of hope or a proof of love. They would not have a tool in their hands five minutes without discovering its purpose, but they live their *lives* without ever having inquired their meaning. Having no reason for living, suffering embitters them, poisons them, and finally, the great door of life's opportunity is closed in their faces, and like the thief on the left they go out into the night unblessed.

Now look at the thief on the right—the symbol of those for whom pain has a meaning. At first he did not understand it, and therefore joined in the curses with the thief on the left. But just as sometimes a flash of lightning will illumine the path we have missed, so too the Savior's forgiveness of His executioners illumined for the thief the road of mercy. He began to see that if pain had no reason Jesus would not have embraced it. If the cross had no purpose Jesus would not have climbed it. Surely He Who claimed to be God would never have taken that badge of shame unless it could be transformed and transmuted to some holy purpose. Pain was beginning to be reasonable for the thief; for the present at least it mean an occasion to do penance for his life of crime. The moment that light came to him he rebuked the thief on the left saying: "Neither dost thou fear God, seeing thou art under the same condemnation? And we indeed justly, for we receive the due reward of our deeds; but this man hath done no evil."[113]

Now he saw pain as doing to his soul something like that which fire does to gold: burning away the dross. Or something like that which fever does to disease: killing the germs. Pain was dropping scales away from his eyes; and, turning toward the central cross, he no longer saw a crucified man, but a Heavenly King. Surely, He Who can pray for pardon for His murderers

---

[113] Luke 23:40-41.

will not cast off a thief: "Lord, remember me when thou shalt come into thy kingdom." Such great faith found its reward: "Amen I say to thee, this day thou shalt be with me in paradise."[114]

Pain in itself is not unbearable; it is the failure to understand its meaning that is unbearable. If that thief did not see purpose in pain he would never have saved his soul. Pain can be the death of our soul, or it can be its life. It all depends on whether or not we link it up with Him Who, "having joy set before him, endured the cross".[115] One of the greatest tragedies in the world is wasted pain. Pain without relation to the cross is like an unsigned check—without value. But once we have it countersigned with the Signature of the Savior on the Cross, it takes on an infinite value. A feverish brow that never throbs in unison with a Head crowned with thorns, or an aching hand never borne in patience with a Hand on the Cross, is sheer waste. The world is worse for that pain when it might have been so much the better. All the sick-beds in the world are either on the right side of the Cross or on the left; their position is determined by whether, like the thief on the left, they ask to be taken down, or, like the thief on the right, they ask to be taken up.

It is not so much what people suffer that makes the world mysterious; it is rather how much they miss when they suffer. They seem to forget that even as children they made obstacles in their games in order to have something to overcome. Why, then, when they grow into man's estate, should there not be prizes won by effort and struggle? Can not the spirit of man rise with adversity as the bird rises against the resistance of the wind? Do not the game fish swim upstream? Must not the alabaster box be broken to fill the house with ointment? Must

---

[114] Luke 23:42–43.

[115] Heb. 12:2.

not the chisel cut away the marble to bring out the form? Must not the seed falling to the ground die before it can spring forth into life? Must not the little streams speed into the ocean to escape their stagnant self-content? Must not grapes be crushed that there may be wine to drink, and wheat ground that there may be bread to eat?

Why then cannot pain be made redemption? Why under the alchemy of Divine Love cannot crosses be turned into crucifixes? Why cannot chastisements be regarded as penances? Why cannot we use a cross to become God-like? We cannot become like Him in His Power; we cannot become like him in His Knowledge. There is only one way we can become like Him, and that is in the way He bore His sorrows and His Cross. And that way was with love. "Greater love than this no man hath, that a man lay down his life for his friends."[116] It is love that makes pain bearable. As long as we feel it is doing good for another, or even for our own soul by increasing the glory of God, it is easier to bear. A mother keeps a vigil at the bedside of her sick child. The world calls it "fatigue" but she calls it love.

A little child was commanded by his mother not to walk the picket fence. He disobeyed and fell, maimed himself and was never able to walk again. Being told of his misfortune he said to his mother: "I know I will never walk again; I know it is my own fault; but if you will go on loving me I can stand anything." So it is with our own pains. If we can be assured that God still loves and cares, then we shall find joy even in carrying on His redemptive work—by being redeemers with a small "r" as His is Redeemer with a capital "R". Then will come to us the vision of the difference between Pain and Sacrifice. Pain is sacrifice without love. Sacrifice is pain with love. When we understand

---

[116] John 15:13.

this, then we shall have an answer for those who feel that God should have let us sin without pain:

"The cry of earth's anguish went up unto God,—
　　'Lord, take away pain,—

The shadow that darkens the world Thou has made,
　　The close-coiling chain

That strangles the heart, the burden that weighs
　　On the wings that would soar,—

Lord, take away pain from the world Thou hast made
　　That it love Thee the more.'

"Then answered the Lord to the world He had made,
　　'Shall I take away pain?

And with it the power of the soul to endure
　　Made strong by the strain?

Shall I take away pity that knits heart to heart
　　And sacrifice high?

Will ye lose all your heroes who lift from the flame
　　White brows to the sky?

Shall I take away love that redeems with a price
　　And smiles through the loss,—

Can ye spare from the lives that would climb unto mine
　　The Christ on His Cross?'"[117]

And now this final lesson. You and I often ask God for many favors which are never granted. I can imagine the thief on the right during his life asking God for many favors, and especially

---

[117] George Stewart, *God and Pain* (New York: George H. Duran Company, 1927).

for wealth. On the other hand, though God does not always grant our material favors, there is one prayer He always grants. There is a favor that you and I can ask of God this very moment, if we had the courage to do it, and that favor would be granted before the day is over. That prayer which God has never refused and will never refuse is the prayer for suffering. Ask Him to send you a cross and you will receive it!

But why does He not always answer our prayers for an increase in salary, for larger commissions, for more money? Why did He not answer the prayer of the thief on the left to be taken down from the cross, and why did He answer the prayer of the thief on the right to forgive his sins? Because material favors draw us away from Him, but the cross always draws us to Him. And God does not want the world to have us! He wants us Himself because He died for us!

THE SUFFERING OF
THE INNOCENT

(The Third Word from The Cross)

Address delivered on March 20, 1938

W hy do the innocent suffer? I do not mean the innocent who have suffering involuntarily thrust upon them, but rather those good souls who go out in search of suffering and are impatient until they find a cross. In other words, why should there be Carmelites, Poor Clares, Trappists, and dozens of penitential orders of the Church, who do nothing but sacrifice and suffer for the sins of men? Certainly not because suffering is necessarily connected with personal sin. Our Lord told us that much, when to those who asked concerning a blind boy, "Who hath sinned, this man, or his parents...?", Our Lord answered "Neither".[118]

If we are to find the answer we must go not merely to the suffering of innocent people, but to the suffering of Innocence Itself. In this *Third Word* our attention is riveted upon the two most sinless creatures who ever trod our sinful earth: Jesus and Mary. Jesus Himself was sinless by nature, for He is the all holy Son of God. Mary was sinless by grace, for she is "our tainted nature's solitary boast". And yet both suffer in the extreme. Why did He suffer Who had the power of God to escape the Cross?

---

[118] John 9:2–3.

Why did she suffer who could have dispensed herself because of her virtue, or could have been excused by her Divine Son?

Love is the key to the mystery. Love by its very nature is not selfish, but generous. It seeks not its own, but the good of others. The measure of love is not the pleasure it gives—that is the way the world judges it—but the joy and peace it can purchase for others. It counts not the wine it drinks, but the wine it serves. Love is not a circle circumscribed by self: it is a cross with arms embracing all humanity. It thinks not of having but of being had, not of possessing but of being possessed, not of owning but of being owned.

Love then by its nature is social. Its greatest happiness is to gird its loins and serve at the banquet of life. Its greatest unhappiness is to be denied the joy of sacrifice for others. *That is why in the face of pain, love seeks to unburden the sufferer and take his pain, and that is why in the face of sin, love seeks to atone for the injustice of him who sinned.* Do not mothers grieve because they cannot take the hurt of their little child's wounded finger as their own? Do not fathers take over the debts of wayward sons to expiate their foolishness? What does all this mean but the otherness of love? In fact love is so social it would reject emancipation from pain if the emancipation were for itself alone. Love refuses to accept individual salvation; it never bends over man, as the healthy over the sick, but enters into him to take his very sickness. It refuses to have its eyes clear when other eyes are bedewed with tears; it cannot be happy unless everyone is happy or unless justice is served; it shrinks from isolation and aloofness from the burdens and hungers of others. It spurns insulation from the shock of the world's sorrow, but insinuates itself into them as if the sorrow were its very own.

This is not difficult to understand. Would you want to be the only person in all the world who had eyes to see? Would you want to be the only man who could walk in a universe of the lame? Would you, if you loved your family, stand on the dock and watch them all drown before your very eyes? And if not, why not? Very simply, because you love them, because you feel so much one with them that their heartaches are your own heartbreaks.

Now apply this to Our Lord and His Blessed Mother. Here is love at its peak, and innocence at its best. Can they be indifferent to that which is a greater evil than pain, namely sin? Can they watch humanity carry a cross to the Golgotha of death while they themselves refuse to share its weight? Can they be indifferent to the outcome of love if they themselves *are* Love? If love means identification and sympathy with the one loved, then why should not God so love the world as to send His only begotten Son into it to redeem the world? And if that Divine Son loved the world enough to die for it, why should not the Mother of Love Incarnate share that redemption? If human love suffers with the pain of the one loved, why should not Divine Love suffer when it comes to contact with sin in the one loved? If mothers suffer in their children, if a husband grieves in the sorrow of his wife, and if friends feel the agony of their beloved's cross, why should not Jesus and Mary suffer in the humanity they love and of which they are the head? If you would die for your family of which you are the head, why should not He die for humanity of which He is the Head? And if the deeper the love the more poignant the pain, why should not the Crucifixion be born of that Love? If a sensitive nerve is touched it registers pain in the brain; and since Our Lord is the Head of suffering humanity He felt every sin of every man as His own. That is why the Cross was inevitable. He could not love us perfectly unless He died for us. And His Mother could not love Him perfectly unless she shared that death. That is why His life was given for us, and her heart broken for us; and that too is why He is Redeemer and she is Redemptrix—because they love.

In order more completely to reveal that a Cross was made up of the juncture of Love and sin, Our Lord spoke His *Third Word* to His Mother: "Woman, behold they son"! He did not call her "Mother" but "Woman"; except when addressing John the next moment He added: "[Son] Behold thy mother." The term "Woman" indicated a wider relationship to all humanity than "Mother". It meant that she was to be not only His Mother, but that she was also to be the Mother of all men, as He was the Savior of all men. She was now to have many children—not according to the flesh, but according to the spirit. Jesus was her first born of the flesh in joy; John was her second born of the spirit in sorrow; and we her millionth and millionth born. If she loved Him Who died for all men, then she must love those for whom He died. That was His clear, unmistakable meaning. The love of neighbor is inseparable from the love of God. His love had no limits; He died for every man. Her love then must have no limits. It must not be merely unselfish; it must even be social. She must be the Mother of every man. An earthly mother loves her own children most, but Jesus is now telling her that even John is her son too, and John was the symbol of all of us. The Father did not spare His Son, nor did the Son spare His Mother, for love knows no bounds. Jesus had a sense of responsibility for every soul in the world; Mary too, inspired by His love, had a corresponding sense of responsibility. If He would be the Redeemer of the wayward children, she must be their Mother.

Now does that throw any light on the problem? Why do innocent, pure, good souls leave the world and its pleasures, feast on fasts, embrace the Cross, and pray their hearts out? The answer is, *because they love.* "Greater love than this no man hath, that a man lay down his life for his friends." They love the world so much they want to save it, and they know there is no other way to save it than to die for it. Many of us so love the world that we live *in* it and are *of* it, but in the end do nothing *for* it. Wrong indeed are they who say these innocent victims hate the world. As soon as the world hears of a beautiful young woman or an upright young man entering the religious life, it asks: "Why did they leave the world?" They left the world, not because they hated the world, but because they loved it. They love the world with its human souls so much that they want to do all they can for it; and they can do nothing better for it than to pray that souls may one day find their way to God.

Our Lord did not hate the world; it hated Him. But He loved it. Neither do they hate the world; they are in love with it and everyone in it. They so much love the sinners in it that they expiate for their sins; they so much love the Communists in it that they bless them as they send them to their God; they so much love the atheists in it that they are willing to surrender the joy of the divine presence that the atheist may feel less afraid in the dark. They are so much lovers of the world that they may be said to be organic with it. They know that things and souls are so much interrelated that what the good one does has repercussion on the millions, just as ten just men could have saved Sodom and Gomorrah. If a stone is thrown into the sea it causes a ripple which widens in ever greater circles until it affects even the most distant shore; a rattle dropped from a baby's crib affects even the most distant star; a finger is burnt and the whole body feels the pain. The cosmos then is organic; but so also is humanity. We are all called to be members of a great family. God is Our Father, Who sent His Son into the world to be Our Brother, and He on the Cross asked Mary to be Our Mother. Now if in the human body it is possible to graft skin from one member to another, why is it not possible also to graft prayer? If it is possible to transfuse blood, why is it not possible also to transfuse sacrifice? Why cannot the innocent atone for the sinful? Why cannot the real lovers of souls, who refuse to be emancipated from sorrow, do for the world what Jesus did on the Cross and Mary did beneath it? The answer to this question has filled the cloisters.

No one on earth can measure the good these divine lovers are doing for the world. How often have they stayed the wrath of a righteous God! How many sinners have they brought to the confessional! How many death-bed conversions have they effected! How many persecutions have they averted? We do not know, and they do not want to know, so long as love wins over hate. But let us not be foolish and ask: What good do they do for the world? We might as well ask: What good did the Cross do?

After all, only the innocent can understand what sin is. No one until the time of Our Lord ever thought of giving his life to save sinners, simply because no one was sinless enough to know its horrors. We who have familiarized ourselves with it become used to it, as a leprous patient after many years of suffering cannot wholly appreciate the evil of leprosy. Sin has lost its horror; we never think of correlating it to the cross; we never advert to its repercussions on humanity.

> "Vice is a monster of so frightful mein,
>   As to be hated, needs but to be seen;
>   Yet seen too oft, familiar with her face,
>   We first endure, then pity, then embrace."[119]

---

[119] Samuel Johnson, ed., *The Poetical Works of Alexander Pope, Esq.* (Philadelphia: J.J. Woodward, 1839).

The best way to know sin is by not sinning. But Jesus and Mary were wholly innocent—He by nature, she by grace; therefore they could understand and know the evil of sin. Having never compromised with it, there were now no compromises to be made. It was something so awful that to avoid it or to atone for it they shrink not even from a death on the cross.

But by a peculiar paradox, though innocence hates sin, because it alone knows its gravity, it nevertheless loves the sinner. Jesus loved Peter who fell three times, and Mary chose as her companion at the foot of the cross, a converted prostitute. What must the scandal mongers have said of that friendship as they watched Mary and Magdalen ascend and descend the hill of Calvary? But Mary braved it all, in order that in a future generation you and I might have hope in her as the "Refuge of sinners". Let there be no fear that she cannot understand our sinful misery because she is Immaculate, for if she had Magdalen as a companion then, why can she not have us now?

Dear Mother Immaculate, but seldom in history have the innocent suffered as they do today. Countless Marys and Johns stand beneath the cross for no other crime than that they loved the Man on the Cross. If there be no remission of sins without the shedding of blood, then let these innocent victims of hate in Russia, in Spain, and in Mexico, be the redemption of those who hate. We ask not that the hateful perish; we only ask that the sufferings of the just be the salvation of the wicked.

Thou didst suffer innocently because thou didst love us in union with they Divine Son. Thus were we taught that only those who cease to love ever flee from the Cross. The innocents who hare slaughtered are no longer the babes of Bethlehem; they are the grown-up children of God—men and women who save the Church today as Bethlehem's babes once saved Jesus. Be thou their consolation, their joy, their Mother, O Innocent Woman who binds the sons of men to the Sons of God in the unity of the Father and the Holy Ghost, world without end, Amen.

⚖️ MORAL SUFFERING

(The Fourth Word From The Cross)

Address delivered on March 27, 1938

The first three *Words* on the cross have reference to physical suffering: this *Fourth Word* has reference to moral suffering or sin. Physical suffering is pain; moral suffering is evil or sin. Our world takes sin very lightly, regarding it too often as a relic of ages which were ignorant of evolution and psychoanalysis. It is the contrary which is true: the more we know about death and its causes the more we know about sin, for in the language of Sacred Scripture, "the wages of sin is death".[120] Death and sin are identified and rightly so: death in the physical order corresponds to evil in the moral order. Death in the physical order is normally the domination of a lower order over a higher order. For example, animals and men generally die through the slow oxidation and burning out of the organism. At that moment, when the oxidation of the chemical order dominates the biological order, the phenomenon called death ensues.

Now man has not only a body, but also a soul. At that precise point, then, when the lower law of self dominates the higher law of charity, when the flesh dominates the spirit, when the love of earth gains supremacy over the love of God, there is the subversion of due order, and that domination of the lower over

---

[120] Rom. 6:23.

the higher order we call sin. What death is to the body, that sin is to the soul, namely the surrender of life—human in one case, divine in the other. That is why St. Paul calls sin a crucifixion or the killing of the divine life within us: Know you not that as often as you sin, you crucify Christ anew in your hearts.

Since sin is the taking of divine life, it follows that nowhere else was sin better revealed than on Calvary, for there sinful humanity crucified the Son of God in the flesh. Here sin comes to a burning focus. It manifests itself in its essence: the taking of Divine Life. Moral evil reaches its greatest power in taking of the life of the Man of Sorrows, for a world capable of killing the God-man is capable of doing anything. Nothing else it can ever do will be worse, and all that it will ever do will be but the re-enactment of this tragedy. There, where character was perfect, and suffering most undeserved, the victory of evil was most complete.

If sin could have found a reason for being vengeful towards God, the crime would have been less heinous. But His enemies could find no fault in Him except His all-compassing Goodness. But goodness is the one thing sin cannot endure, for goodness is sin's constant reproach. The wicked always hate the good. The very unreasonableness of the judgment against Our Lord—for even Pilate admitted he found the Man innocent—was the mirror of the anarchy of sin. Sin chose the battleground, set up the gallows of torture, influenced the judges, inflamed the crowds, and decided on the death of Divine Life. It could have chosen no better way of revealing its nature. It refused to have God on earth, and so it lifted His Cross above the earth. Sin wanted no shepherding calls to repentance, and so it fastened Him to a tree. "He came unto his own, and his own received him not."[121]

---

[121] John 1:11.

They abandoned Him at birth: they would now abandon Him in death. Thus would sin reach its most perfect expression: for *sin is the abandonment of God by man.*

But the Savior is on the Cross not to go down to defeat, but to redeem from sin. How better can He atone for sin than by taking upon Himself one of its most bitter consequences? Since sin is the abandonment of God by man, He now wills to feel the abandonment of man by God. Such is the meaning of the *Fourth Word* uttered in the moment when darkness crept over Calvary like a leprosy: "My God, my God, why hast thou abandoned me?"[122] Man rejected Himself. Man turned away from God; He, Who was ever united with God, now wills to feel that awful wrench, as if He Himself were guilty. It was all deliberate. He was laying His life down of Himself, even when they thought they were taking it away. He willed to be identified with man, and now He resolves to travel the road to the end and to take upon Himself the terrible loneliness of sin. His pain of abandonment expressed in this *Fourth Word* was double: the abandonment by man and God. Man abandoned Him because He clings to God in His Prayer; God seemingly abandons Him because He wills to forego divine consolation to taste the bitter dregs of sin that the cup of sin may empty. As a symbol of that double abandonment by heaven and earth, His cross is suspended between both, and yet uniting them for the first time since Adam abandoned God. None of us knows the deeper meaning of the cry; no one can know. He alone Who is sinless can know the utter horror of sin which caused it.

But this we do know, that at this moment He permitted Himself to feel the solitariness and abandonment caused by sin. And yet His cry proves that though men do abandon

---

[122] Mark 15:34.

Him they never completely desert Him, for a man can no more shake off God than he can deny parentage. That is why His cry of abandonment was prefaced with the cry of belief; "My God, my God!" Into it was concentrated the loneliness of every sinful heart that ever lived, and yet with it all was the divine nostalgia—the loneliness of the atheist who says there is no God and yet under starry skies believes in His Power; the loneliness of fallen-away Catholics, who have left the Church not for reasons but for things, and who like prodigal children still dream of the happiness of the servants in the Father's house; the loneliness of the enemies of religion who testify to its reality by the bitterness of their hate, for no man hates a mirage; the loneliness of the pessimists who complain against the evil in the world, but only because they believe more deeply still in the reality of Justice; the loneliness of sinners who hate themselves for hating virtue; the loneliness of the worldly who live without religion, not because they deny it but because they are "sore adread lest, having Him, [they] should have enough beside."[123] All in their own way are saying: "I abandon and yet I believe." It is just that which makes one wonder if there is really any sinner who has ever gone so far down its dark, damp corridors as to forget that he left the light. The words on the cross seem to say so much. Not even those direct descendants of the executioners who pillage churches and crucify Christ's ambassadors have yet proved it, for how can one hate so intensely that which he believes to be only a dream? If religion is the opium of the people, why, instead of putting men to sleep, does it awaken them to martyrdom? There is no explanation; only the Infinite can be infinitely hated and infinitely loved. That is why sinners

---

[123] *The Hound of Heaven.*

crucified Our Lord, and why the crucifixion made saints. Our Lord is the Infinite God.

It is hard for us to grasp the awfulness of sin, but if we cannot see it in its relation to the death of the all-holy One of God, then we are beyond repentance. The truth is that as long as sin endures, the Crucifixion endures. Clovis, the King of the Franks, on hearing for the first time the story of the Crucifixion said: "If I had been there with my army, this never would have happened." But the fact is, Clovis was there. So was his army. So were we. The Crucifixion atoned not only for the sins of the past but also for the sins of the future.

"I saw the Son of God go by
 Crowned with a crown of thorns.
'Was it not finished Lord' said I,
'And all the anguish borne?'

"He turned on me His awful eyes,
'Hast thou not understood?
 Lo, every soul is a Calvary
 And every sin a rood!'"[124]

Because our body seems closer to us than our soul, we are apt to think of pain as being a greater evil than sin. But such is not the case: "Fear ye not them that kill the body ... but rather fear him that can destroy both soul and body in hell."[125]

Thus the reality of sin in the Crucifixion and the idea of Hell become related. The Cross proves that life is fraught with tremendous issues; that sin is so terrible that full payment in justice could be made only by the death of God-made-man.

---

[124] Rachel A. Taylor, *The Question*.

[125] Mark 10:28.

If sin cost the death of Divine Life, then the refusal to accept Redemption can mean nothing less than eternal death or Hell.

Life then is not a mere experience; it is a drama which involves issues of Eternal Life and Eternal Death. Those who would rob justice of Hell would rob Christ of His Cross. Were we but animals, our choices would pass away with their fulfillment, but just as our thoughts are fastened to Truth which is unchangeable, so too our resolves are registered on the scroll of Perfect Goodness which is eternal. If in our business we take from our cash registers the slip on which is recorded the debits and credits of the day, shall we be so unreasonable to believe that we, who live by such an order, should ourselves be governed any differently? Why then at the end of our day's work on earth should not the Divine Bookkeeper find registered on our conscience our answer to the question of whether our life has been a failure or a success? Either we lose our soul or we find it; either we live or we die. And if such a fate does not come at the end of our story, then the Cross is a mockery and life is vain. But seeing how high we can rise and how low we can fall, we can see the importance of our choices—the danger of being careless and the thrill of being brave. As one writer has put it, "They are cowards who educate us to think that we are meant to stop at home in swaddling clothes, protected from fresh air and all possible dangers. They would make us soft and effeminate and unfit for the hurly-burly of life. This is no man's life but a tame travesty of it. All that is best in us revolts against coddling and the denial of all risk and adventure. What we need is some summons to the semi-divine courage which is latent in all of us, some challenge to risk all that we have for love. Imagine a man born of woman, ambling along on some old nag or wrapped up in some limousine to conquer the earth and to conquer himself and to make himself fit for the Divine Eros. I am tired of this cheapening of stupendous issues; I demand that Hell be given back to world".[126] And if it be not given back to the world, then men will say, no matter how foul we become, all will be well with us in the end. But as long as Hell remains we have a standard by which evil can be judged, by which those who trample the love of man and God underfoot can be measured, by which those who attempt to drive God from the earth He made can be weighed. If a man wants to know his worth let him take one look at the Man on the Cross. There Love stands Crucified! If he crucified Love, then he is without love; and to be without Love is Hell! If he crucifies his lower self to be Christ-like, then he is in love, and to be in love with Love is heaven.

> *Dear Savior, open our eyes to see that our forgetfulness of the horror of sin is the beginning of our ruin. Too prone are we to blame finances, economics, and balances of trade for our ills, our woes; too unmindful are we that these are but the symptoms of our rebellion against Thy Divine Law. Because we have rebelled against Thee, Our Creator, creatures have turned against one another, and the world becomes one vast charnal house of hate and envy. Give us light to see, O Lord, that it was sin which hardened itself into Thy nails, wove itself into Thy thorns, and congealed itself into Thy Cross. But let us also see that if Thou didst take the Cross for us, then we must be worth saving: for if the Cross is the measure of our sin then the Crucifix is the pledge of our redemption, through the same Christ Our Lord, Amen.*

---

[126] Martin Cyril D'Arcy, S.J., *The Pain of this World* (London: Longmans, Green and Co., 1936), 129.

THE NEED OF ZEAL
(The Fifth Word From The Cross)

Address delivered on March 27, 1937

The *Fourth Word* is the suffering of the soul without God; the *Fifth Word* is the suffering of God without the soul. The cry, "I thirst", refers not to physical thirst, for He refused the draughts they offered Him. It was His soul that was burning and His Heart that was on fire. He was thirsting for the souls of men. The Shepherd was lonely without His sheep; the Creator was yearning for His creatures; the First Born was looking for His brethren.

All during his life He had been searching for souls. He left heaven to find them among the thorns; it mattered little if they made a crown of them for Him, so long as He could find the one that was lost. He said He came "not to call the just, but sinners",[127] and His Heart thirsted for them now more than ever. He could not be happy until every sheep and every lamb was in His sheep-fold. "Other sheep I have, that are not of this fold: them also I must bring ... and there shall be one fold and one shepherd."[128] There was sorrow in His sad complaint during life: "You will not come to me"; but there is tragedy in the last cry: "I thirst."

---

[127] Mark 2:17.

[128] John 10:16.

There was probably no moment during the three hours of redemption in which Our Lord suffered more than in this. Pains of the body are nothing compared to the agonies of the soul. Taking His life did not mean so much to Him, for He was really laying it down of Himself. But for man to spurn His love—that was enough to break His Heart. It is difficult for us to grasp the intensity of this suffering, simply because none of us ever love enough. We have not the capacity for love that He has, therefore we can never miss it so much when it is denied. But where our tiny little hearts are sometimes denied the love they crave, we do get some faint inkling of what must have gone on in His Own great Heart. The faithful loyal wife whose husband is snatched from her by death, the mother whose son refuses to visit her and bless her declining days with filial affection, the friend who has sacrificed all only to be betrayed by one for whom he gave all—all these experiences the keenest and bitterest of all human sufferings: the pangs of unrequited love. Such victims can and really do die of a broken heart.

But what is this love for another human being, compared to the love of God for man? The affection a human heart bears for another lessens as it multiplies the objects of its love, just as a river loses its fullness the more it divides itself into little streams. But with God there is no decrease of love with the increase of objects loved, any more than a voice loses its strength because a thousand ears hear it. Each human heart can break His Sacred Heart all over again; each soul has within itself the potentiality of another crucifixion. No one can love as much as Our Lord; no one therefore can suffer as much. Added to this was the fact that His infinite Mind saw within that second all the unfaithful hearts that would ever live until the end of time; all who would follow like Judas, and then betray; all who would fall and refuse His helping Hand; in a word, all who would pass by His Cross and only stop with the executioners to shake dice for His garments, while within a stone's throw of them would be the Prize so precious it was worth gambling their very lives away. It was this picture of ungrateful men which renewed the Agony of the Garden and caused His Death. He died of thirst in the desert of human hearts!

From this *Word* we discover this great lesson: the necessity of our loving our fellow men as Our Lord loves us. If Jesus Christ thirsted for souls, must not a Christian also thirst? If He came to cast fire upon the earth, must not a Christian be enkindled? If He came to bring us the seed of life, must not that seed fructify and bear fruit? If He lit a light in our minds, must we not be illumined? Has He not called us to be His Apostles and His Ambassadors, in order that His Incarnation might be prolonged through the continued dispensation of the divine through the human? A Christian, then, is a man to whom Our Lord has given other men. He breaks bread to the poor through our hands, He consoles the sick through our lips, He visits the sorrowful upon our feet. He sees the fields of harvest through our eyes, and He gathers the bundles into His everlasting barns through our toil. When we fail in our apostolate the failing might be said to be His.

To be worthy of the name Christian, then, means that we too must thirst for the spread of the Divine Love; and if we do not thirst, then we shall never be invited to sit down at the Banquet of Life. Crowns shall be given only to the victors, and the chalice of everlasting wine only to those who thirst. A Catholic who does not strive to spread his Faith is a parasite on the Life of the Church; he who is not girding his loins for apostolate, is abdicating his seat on the dais of Christianity; he who is not bearing fruit is like a tree cut down on the road impeding the march of the army of God; he who is not a conquering spirit is a renegade. The torch of Faith has been given to us not to delight our eyes but to enkindle the torches of our fellow men. Unless we burn and are on fire for the Divine Cause a glacial invasion will sweep the earth which will be the end, for "The Son of man, when he cometh, shall he find, think you, faith on earth?"[129]

The measure of our apostolate is the intensity of our love. A human heart loves to talk about the object of its love, and loves to hear that object praised. If we love Our Lord, then we will love to talk about His Holy Cause for "out of the abundance of the heart the mouth speaketh".[130] To those who have such love, there is never the excuse of a want of opportunity. Our Lord has told us "the harvest indeed is great, but the laborers are few".[131] To the zealous Christian every country is a mission country; every banquet room a Simon's house where another Magdalen can be found; every ship another bark of Peter from which nets of salvation can be let down; every crowded city street another Tyre and Sidon where the whelps that eat the crumbs from the master's table can be rewarded for their faith; and every cross is a throne where thieves become courtiers.

I know there are those that would destroy every mark of the Savior's feet from the face of the earth; I know there are those who would renew the Crucifixion by hating those who preach His love; I know the wicked today hide not the shame of their sins, but seek to find others and make others like unto themselves, in order to find consolation in their corporate decadence. But these are not reasons why Christians should go into the catacombs and leave the earth to the race of Cain. While these enemies of Divine Love live, they are still purchasable by Divine Grace

---

[129] Luke 18:8.

[130] Matt. 12:34.

[131] Matt. 9:37.

and are potential children of the Kingdom of God. They are our opportunities. Our Lord thirsted for them on the Cross, and we must thirst for them too, and love them enough to try to save them. One thing is certain, we are not called to be Christians to damn them, but to save them, in order that all men might be one great redeemed humanity and Christ its Sacred Heart.

Some will always resist, but there are no hopeless cases. Recently in Spain two hundred men were ordered shot when the Spanish people won over a city from the forces of anarchy. These two hundred men had burned churches, murdered priests and nuns, ravaged virgins, and were now to expiate their crimes. The Carmelites who had suffered from their hands began a novena of prayer and fasting, that they might be converted to God before their death. Out of the two hundred, one hundred and ninety-eight at the end of the novena received the Sacraments and died in peace with their Savior.

Something we must never forget is that every man wants to be happy, but he cannot be happy without God. Below the surface of every heart, down deep in its secret gardens, is a craving for which it was made, as even the caged bird still retains its love of flying. As the Holy Father put it: "Beneath the ashes of these perverted lives there are to be found sparks which can be fanned into a flame." Even those who hate religion have never really lost it; if they had, they would not hate it so much. The intensity of their hate is the proof of the reality of that which they hate. If they really lost religion, they would not spend all their energy attempting to make everyone else lose theirs; a man who has lost a watch does not go about persuading others to lose their watches. Thus hate is but their vain attempt to despise. That is why we are not to consider them beyond evangelization. They can still be brought back even at the last moment, as the thief, or as Arthur Rimbaud. Here was a man who blasphemed Christ intensely in his life in his writing; a man whose greatest thrill was to intoxicate anyone who spoke to him of God and Our Lady in order to berate and even physically abuse him. He even delighted in breaking his mother's heart to whom he wrote: "Happily this life is the only one; which is obvious, because one cannot imagine another life with more boredom in it than this one."[132] Then came his end, which is described for us in the language of François Mauriac:

> "Now imagine a human being who has great powers of resistance, who is much more masterful than I am, and who hates this servitude. Imagine a nature irritated and exasperated to distraction by this mysterious servitude and finally delivered over to an abandoned hatred of the cross. He spits on this sign which he drags after him and assures himself that the bonds which attach him to it could never stand out against a methodical and planned degradation of his soul and spirit. Thus he cultivates blasphemy and perfects it as an art and fortifies his hatred of sacred things with an armor of scornful contempt. Then suddenly, above this stupendous defilement, a voice rises, complainingly, appealingly; it is hardly so much as a cry, and no sooner has the sky received it than the echo is smothered by frightful jeers and by the laugh of the devil. As long as this man is strong enough, he will drag this cross as a prisoner his ball-chain, never accepting it. He will obstinately insist on wearing this wood along all the paths of the world. He will choose the lands of fire and ashes most suited to consume it. However heavy the cross becomes, it will not exhaust his hatred until the fateful day, the turning-point in his destiny, when he sinks down at last under the weight of the tree and under its agonizing embrace.

---

[132] François Mauriac, *God and Mammon* (London: Sheed & Ward, 1936).

He still writhes, pulls himself together and then sinks down again, hurling out a last blasphemy. From his hospital bed he brings abominable accusations against the nuns who are tending him; he treats the angelic sister as a fool and an idiot and then, at last, he breaks off. This is the moment marked from all eternity. The cross which has dragged him for thirty-seven years and which he has denied and covered with spittle offers its arms to him: the dying man throws himself upon it, presses it to him, clings to it, embraces it; he is serenely sad and heaven is in his eyes. His voice is heard: 'Everything must be prepared in my room, everything must be arranged. The chaplain will come back with the Sacraments. You will see. They're going to bring the candles and the lace. There must be white linen everywhere....."[133]

No! Religion is not the opium of the people. Opium is the drug of deserters who are afraid to face the Cross—the opiate that gives momentary escape from the Hound of Heaven in pursuit of the human soul. Religion, on the contrary, is the elixir which spurs a soul on to the infinite goal for which it was made. Religion supplies the profoundest desires. The greatest thirst of all is the thirst of unrequited love—the hand reached out which never grasps; the arms outstretched which never embrace; the hands knocking on a door which is never opened. It is these things religion satisfies by making man think less about his passing desires and more about his ultimate desire. His passing desires are multiple and fleeting—gold one minute, food another, pleasure another. But his ultimate desire is unique and abiding—the perfect happiness of everlasting joy and peace. It is our duty to lead men to the realization of this desire. Those who hate religion are seeking religion; those who wrongly condemn

---

[133] *Ibid.*, 41.

are still seeking justice; those who overthrow order are seeking a new order; even those who blaspheme are adoring their own gods—but still adoring. From certain points of view they are all prisoners of Divine Love; they are confusing desires with *the* desire, passions with love. They are all living in the shadow of the Cross, they are all thirsting for the Fountain of Divine Life. Their lips were made to drink—and we must not refuse to give them to drink.

A PLANNED
UNIVERSE

(The Sixth Word From The Cross)

Address delivered on April 3, 1938

In the face of the undeserved suffering of the just, and the unmerited prosperity of the wicked, and the misery of the merciful, many are wont to ask this question: Is this a planned universe, or is it the plaything of chance?

This question would have been unanswerable in this life had not Goodness itself descended to the level of the world's woe, deliberately and willfully. But once the Best freely goes down to the worst, and fits it into His plan and purpose, then no man can ever be without hope. If a man who knows nothing about electricity is told that a bolt of electricity more powerful than lightening is to be released by a scientist in a small laboratory, that man will not fear the result so long as he is certain that the scientist knows what he is doing. He reasons that the scientist understands the nature of electricity. If he hurls that otherwise destructive fire in a tiny room, it must be because he knows how to control its force. In other words, he has a plan or purpose. In like manner, if God, Who could have foregone the trials and sorrows of man, by a free act descends to man, assumes his nature, and unites it with His Own Divine Nature, and then with eyes open and with full knowledge of the world's iniquity, walks into it and even embraces it, it must be because it fits into His Divine pattern.

Our Blessed Lord did not walk blindly into a world capable of crucifying virtue, as you and I might walk into an unknown forest. He came into it as a doctor into his hospital with full knowledge of how to deal with pain. His whole course was charted beforehand: nothing took Him by surprise. At any given moment He had the Power to overcome, but He would not use the Power regardless of how much He was challenged until He *willed* it. It is this Divine knowledge which explains His rejoinder to Mary and Joseph in the temple, when He was only twelve years of age: "Did you not know that I must be about my Father's business?"[134] Already He talks of a plan, and in particular of a plan that is made in heaven. It also explains His many prophecies concerning His death, its time, its place, and its circumstances, and the almost impatient urge He had to realize it. "I have a baptism wherewith I am to be baptized: and how I am straitened until it be accomplished!"[135] Death then would not be a stumbling block to Him as it was to Socrates for whom it was but an unwanted interruption of his teaching. For Our Lord, death was the goal He was seeking, the supreme objective of His mission on earth. Everyone else who ever came into the world, came into it to live. Our Lord came into it to *die*. But that death with its scourgings and tears would not come to Him in an unguarded moment. Many times during His life when His enemies sought to kill Him, He said His "hour was not yet come." When "the hour" He set did come, He refused the help of heaven and earth to postpone it or escape it. He refused heaven's help for had He not said: "Thinkest thou that

[134] Luke 2:49.

[135] Luke 12:50.

I cannot ask my Father, and he will give me presently more than twelve legions of angels"?[136] He refused earth's help, for He told Peter: "Put up thy sword into the scabbard".[137] His enemies did not come to Him: He went to them. And He went saying: "This is your hour, your hour of darkness. Your hour when I allow you to do with Me whatever you please; the hour when I might turn my back upon the ills of humanity, but in which I drink its chalice of bitterness even to its very dregs." He "having joy set before him, endured the cross".[138] Bodily suffering, mental anguish, bitter disappointment, the false judgment of justice, the betrayal of true friendship, the court's perversion of honesty, and the violent separation from a mother's love—all these He took upon Himself knowingly, freely, deliberately, and purposely. Then after three hours of crucifixion, surveying all the prophecies made about Him in Old Testament days, and the prophecies He had made of Himself, and seeing them all fulfilled and the last stitch drawn on the tapestry of His life and the pattern completed, He uttered His *Sixth Word*—a word of triumph: "It is finished."

That cry meant: This is a planned universe. Suffering fits into it, otherwise He would have refused it. The cross fits into it, otherwise He would not have embraced it. The crown of thorns fits into it, otherwise He would not have worn it. Nothing was accidental; everything was ordered. His Father's business was completed. The plan was finished.

The full significance of the plan was not revealed until three days later, when the Seed which fell to the ground arose into the newness of Life. It was this plan Our Lord gave to the disciple at

---

[136] Matt. 26:53.

[137] John 18:11.

[138] Heb. 12:2.

Emmaus: "Ought not Christ to have suffered these things and so to enter into his glory?"[139] In other words, unless there is a Good Friday in our lives there will never be an Easter Sunday; unless we die to this world, we shall not live to the next; unless there is the crown of thorns, there will never be the halo of light; unless there is the cross, there will never be an empty tomb; unless we lose our life, we shall not find it; unless we are crucified with Christ, we shall never rise with Christ. Such is the plan, and on our choice depends eternal issues. Our attitude toward the inescapable cross immortalizes us, either for gain or loss. And though the plan seems hard, it is not blind, for Our Lord has not merely told us to follow Him—He has led the way. We can follow His footsteps out of the dark forest of our sufferings, but we can never say: He does not know what it means to suffer. He suffered first to teach us how to bear it. He did not say: "Go to the Cross", but He did say: "Come, follow me." Because He was God He knew that men would not go just because they were told, but that they would follow if an example were given.

Our Lord made use of the contradictions of life to redeem us; we must make use of the same contradictions to apply the fruits of that redemption. His plan is finished for He is now enjoying glory. Our plan is not yet finished, for we have not yet saved our souls. But everything we do must be directed to that one supreme goal, for "what doth it profit a man, if he gain the whole world, and suffer the loss of his own soul?"[140] Is not that the reason why in God's plan of the universe suffering generally comes at the end instead of at the beginning? This is a fact. Youth is full of hopes, age is burdened with cares. Paradise came at the beginning of human history, and seven vials of wrath will come

---

[139] Luke 24:26.

[140] Matt. 16:26.

at its end. The angels sang at His birth, but His executioners blasphemed at His death. Even in religion the greatest spiritual joys seem to come at ordination, or at reception of the veil, or at conversion, or at the marriage ceremony. Later on God seems to withdraw His consoling sweetness, as a mother no longer coaxes a grown child with candy, in order to teach us that we must walk on our own feet, and work for the joys beyond.

As reasonable beings, we must ask why suffering, sadness, disillusionment, and cares, all seem to come in the evening of life? The first reason seems to be to remind us that earth is not a paradise, and that the life, truth, and love we crave is not to be found here below. As Abraham was told to go out of his country, so we seem to be told by life's bitterness to go out of ourselves, to look beyond and upwards to the completion of our plan. It is the burn of the fire that makes the child snatch his hand away, and it is the burden and bitterness of life that make us draw ourselves away from earth. God is, as it were, urging us on to *finish* our lives and not merely to have them end, as the animals that rise to eat and then lie down to die.

Then, too, God permits these crosses in the twilight of our lives in order to supply the defects of our love. If we gave our young bones to the world, our sufferings remind us that we can still give our dry bones to God. The crucifixion gave the good thief his one good opportunity for making amends for his failure to love; but the final cross and an act of love purchased Paradise that very day. Too many of us are like St. Augustine, who during the delirious viciousness of his early life, said: "I want to be good, a little later on, dear Lord, but not now." It takes a cross very often to jolt us back again into the plan, just as many mechanical devices are restored to order by a jolt. Life's wrenches and throbs do more than anything else to convince us that we can never find happiness on earth; and if it could be found here, man would never so universally have sought God.

"If there had anywhere appeared in space
  Another place of refuse, where to flee,
  Our hearts had taken refuge in the at place,
  And not with Thee.

"For we against creation's bars had beat
  Like prisoner eagles, through great worlds had sought
  Though but a foot of ground to plant our feet
  Where Thou wert not.

"And only when we found in earth and air
  In Heaven or hell, that such might nowhere be
  That we could not flee from Thee anywhere
  We fled to Thee."[141]

I believe this *Sixth Word* explains that really astounding fact that we have in this life greater capacities for pain than for pleasure. We can enjoy pleasures but if we continue in them abnormally they reach a point where they turn into pain. They do not lead us on and on to richer Elysian fields; rather do they turn back on us and wound us. Even the very repetition of a pleasure dulls the pleasure itself. Tickling begins with laughter and ends with pain.

But with pain it is different. In moments of intense suffering we feel we could not bear it if it continued a minute longer. It goes on beyond that minute and we tap new layers of endurability. But never does pain pass into pleasure. No toothache ever becomes fun just because it lasts a week.

---

[141] Alfred Henry Miles, ed., "Richard Chenevix Trench," in *The Sacred Poets of the Nineteenth Century* (London: George Routledge & Sons, Ltd., 1906), 226.

Now why is it that we have greater resources for pain than for pleasure? The real reason is this: if we live our lives as God intended that we should, then we shall leave pain behind in this world and enjoy everlasting bliss in the next. Pleasure is reserved for the next world; that is why it plays traitor to us here. Pain is not intended for the next world; that is why we can exhaust it here. Pain exists in the next world only for those who refuse to lose their life in order to possess it.

That brings up the supreme importance of the masterpiece of a happy death. Our Lord labored on *His* masterpiece from eternity, for He is the Lamb slain from the beginning of the world. We must labor on ours from the beginning too, for as the tree falls, there it lies. At the moment of death nothing will be useful to me—except God. If I have Him, then I shall recover everything in Him. For that reason a Christian is never in full possession of his life until the day of his death. That is why the Church calls it a "Natalis"—birthday, the birthday into Eternal life. Eternal exile is only for those who made the earth their fatherland.

No masterpiece was ever completed in a day. It takes years for the artist to discipline his mind and hand, and then years again to chisel away the stubbornness of the marble to make the form appear. The greatest masterpiece of all—a Happy Death—must be prepared for by practice. We learn how to die by dying; dying to our selfishness, our pride, our envy, our sloth, a thousand times a day. This is what Our Lord meant when He said: "If any man will come after me, let him ... take up his cross daily, and follow me."[142] We cannot die well unless we practice it. Then when the time comes for the last stroke we shall be skilled in it, we shall not be taken by surprise. Our tower will have been

---

[142] Luke 9:23.

completed; whether it be high or low will matter not. It only matters that we finish the plan Our Lord has given us to do. And may we all, as an old Irish saying has it: "Be in heaven half in hour before the devil knows we're dead."

⚖

ETERNAL FREEDOM

(The Seventh Word From The Cross)

Address delivered on April 10, 1938

F ear ye not them that kill the body ... but rather fear him that can destroy both soul and body in hell."[143] Calvary is wrapped up in these words of Our Blessed Lord, for herein is revealed the supreme struggle of every life, namely the struggle to preserve our spiritual freedom. Sometimes it can be preserved easily, but if it demands the sacrifice of that which is lower, even the sacrifice of our life, we must not fear to make even that surrender. A moment may come in the life of every politician when, in order to keep his independence, he must sacrifice the ease and influence which comes with the bribe. The Christian, in like manner, must prepare to forego even the world in order to be captain of his soul.

This is not just a precept, for our Divine Savior put His words into practice. He kept His soul free at the cost of His life. He went down into slavery in all the inconsequential details of earthly existence in order to be able to call His soul His own. His majesty He surrendered to the supremacy of His enemies: His hands and feet He enslaved to their nails; His body He submitted to their grave; His good name He subjugated to their scorn; His blood He poured forth captive to their lance; His comfort he subjected to their planned pain; and His life He laid down as

---

[143] Matt. 10:28.

a serf at their feet. But His spirit He kept free and for Himself. He would not surrender it, for if He kept His freedom He could recover everything else He had already given into their hands. They knew that, and so they tried to win His Spirit by challenging His Power: "Come down from the cross, and we will believe." If he had power to step down from that Cross, and yet refused, He was not a Crucified Prisoner, but their Judge on his Judgment Seat and their King on His Throne. If He had the power to come down and did come down, then He would have been powerless, for His great strength would have been only exhibitionism and a slave of their weak and taunting jibes. And so Our Lord refused to do the human thing, namely, to come down from the Cross. He did the divine thing and stayed there! By so doing He kept His soul His own. Therefore He could do with it whatever He pleased. All during His life He did the things that were pleasing to His Heavenly Father; now He would do them at His death. Laying hold of His spirit, for He was master of Himself, He sent it back again to His Father, not with a hoarse cry of rebellion, not with a weak murmur of stoical endurance, not with the quivering uncertain tones of a Hamlet debating "to be or not to be", but with the loud, strong, triumphant voice of One Who was free to go to whom He pleased and willed to go only back home: "Father, into thy hands I commend my spirit."

That was the one, inescapable, untouchable thing in His life and every life, the spirit. We can hammer iron, because it is material; we can melt ice, because we can warm it with our fires; we can break twigs, because we can get them into our hands; but we cannot crucify Faith, we cannot melt Hope, we cannot break Charity, and we cannot murder Justice, because all these things are spiritual and therefore beyond the power of enslavement. In a higher sense, the soul of every man is the last and impregnable fortress of character. As long as he wills to keep his spirit his own, no one can take it away, even though they take his life. That spirit he can freely give away or sell for example into the slavery of drink, but it is his own as long as he chooses to keep it. Our Lord kept his free at the most terrible of all costs, to remind us that not even the fear of a crucifixion is a reason for stepping down from the most glorious of all liberties—the power to give our soul to God.

Unfortunately, freedom has lost its value for the modern world. It understands freedom too often as the right to do whatever you please, or the absence of constraint. This is not freedom but license, and often anarchy. Freedom means not the right to do what you *please*, but the right to do what we *should* in order to attain the highest and noblest ends of our nature. An aviator is free not when he disregards the law of gravitation because it suits his fancy, but when he obeys it in order to conquer it and fly. Liberty, then is a means, not an end; not a city, but a bridge. When we say, "We want to be free," the obvious question is, "Free from what?" Free from interruption? "Very well, but why?" "Because I want to travel to a certain place where I have business." Then freedom becomes meaningful. It implies a knowledge of a goal or a purpose.

Now human nature has a goal, namely, the using of this world as a stepping stone to the perfection of our personality in the way of perfect happiness. But if we never stop to ask ourselves why we are here, or where we are going, or what is the purpose of life, then we are changing our direction but we are not making progress; neither are we free. If we forget our real destiny we cut up our lives into tiny, successive, and incomplete destinies, like a man who is lost in a forest, going first one way and then another. If he had a single distant point, say a church steeple, beyond and outside the forest, he would be free either to go out of the forest or remain in it, and he would be making progress as he approached the church steeple. So it is with life: If we have a fixed goal then we can make progress toward it; but it is sheer nonsense to say we are making progress if we constantly change our goal. As long as the model remains fixed, we are free to paint it, but if the model one moment is a rose and the next moment a nose, then art has lost not only its freedom but its joy.

This last and final *Word* on the Cross reminds us that Our Lord never lost sight of His goal; and because He did not, He sacrificed everything else to keep Himself free to attain it. Surplus baggage must often be dropped in order to freely run to refuge. That is why Our Lord told the rich man to leave his bags of gold behind for thus He could more perfectly run the course to eternal life. Our Lord Himself dropped everything, even His life. But He dropped it as a seed into the ground and picked it up again in the freshness of the risen life of Easter Sunday.

From this sacrifice of His life in order to keep His Spirit free for the Father, we must learn not to be overcome by the sorrows and trials and disappointments of life. The danger is that forgetting the ideal, we may concentrate more on saving our body than on saving our soul. Too often we blame persons and things for being indifferent to our pains and aches, as if they were primary. We want nature to suspend its sublime tasks, or we want persons to leave their round of duties, not just to minister to us in our necessities but to soften us with their sympathy. Forgetting that sometimes the work is more than the comfort, we become like those sick at sea who feel the ship should stop, hundreds should be delayed, and the port be forgotten, just to minister to their sickness. Our Blessed Lord on the Cross might have made all nature minister to His wounds, He might have turned the Crown of thorns into a garland of roses, His nails into a scepter, His blood into royal purple, His Cross into a golden throne, His wounds into glittering jewels, but that would have meant the ideal of sitting at the right hand of the Father in His Glory was secondary to an immediate and temporary earthly comfort. Then the purpose of life would have been less important than a moment in it; then the freedom of His Spirit would have been secondary to the healing of His Hands; then the higher self would have been the slave of the lower self—and that is the one thing we are bidden to avoid.

"God strengthen me to bear myself
That heaviest weight of all to bear
Inalienable weight of care.

"All others are outside myself
I lock my door and the bar them out,
The turmoil, tedium, gad-about.

"I lock my door upon myself,
And bar them out; but who shall bar
Self from myself, most loathed of all?

"If I could set aside myself
And start with lightened hear upon
The road by all men overgone!

"God harden me against myself
This coward with pathetic voice
Who craves for ease, and rest, and joys.

"Myself arch-traitor to myself
My hollowest friend, my deadliest foe
My clog whatever road I go.

"Yet One there is can curb myself
Can roll the strangling load from me
Break off the yoke and set me free."[144]

---

[144] Christina G. Rossetti, "Who shall deliver me?", *Poems* (1876).

There is no escaping the one thing necessary in the Christian life, namely saving our souls and purchasing the glorious liberty of the children of God. The crucifixion ends, but Christ endures. Sorrows pass, but we remain. Therefore we must never come down from the supreme end and purpose of life, the salvation of our souls. Ofttimes the temptation will be strong and the temporal advantages will seem so great; but at those moments we must recall the great difference between the solicitation of a sinful pleasure and the appeal of our heavenly destiny. Before we have a sinful pleasure it is attractive and appealing. After we have it, it is disgusting. It was not worth the price; we feel we were cheated and that we sold ourselves out of all proportion to our due worth, as Judas sold the Savior for thirty pieces of silver. But with the spiritual life it is different. Before we have intimate union with Christ and His Cross it seems so distasteful, contrary to our nature, so hard and so uninviting; but after we have given ourselves over to Him it gives a peace and a joy which surpasses all understanding. That is why so many miss Him and His joy. They stand so far away they never learn to know Him. Like the poet they ask:

"Must Thou, Designer Infinite,
Char the wood ere Thou canst limn with it?"[145]

Must the wood be subject to fire before we can paint with it as charcoal? Is death the condition of life? Is the discipline of study the path to knowledge? Are long hours of tedious practice the road to the thrill of music? Must we lose our lives in time in order to save them for eternity? Yes, that is the answer.

But it is not as hard as it seems, for as St. Paul tells us: "the sorrows of this life are not worthy to be compared to the joys

---

[145] *The Hound of Heaven.*

that are to come." How often as little children, when our little toys were broken, we thought life was no longer worth living for the universe was in ruins; and then, surveying the wreck which seemed so hopeless, we cried ourselves to sleep. May not those once great sorrows which faded into insignificance with maturity be but the symbol of the trivialities of our present burdens compared to the joys which await us in the mansions of the Father's House? Only let us not be fooled by those who say human life has no purpose, and who, in the language of a scientist, say that life is like a lit candle and that when the candle is done the flame goes out, and that is the end of us all. But what this scientist forgot to tell us is that light is not something in the candle, but something which emanates from it; something associated with matter but separable and distinct from it. For even when the candle has burned out, the light continues to emit itself at the rate of 186,000 miles a second, beyond the moon and stars, beyond the Pleiades, the nebulas of Andromeda, and continues to do so as long as the universe endures. And so when the candle of our life burns low, may we have kept our soul so free that like a flame it will leap upwards to the Great Fire at which it was enkindled, and never stop until its light meets that Heavenly Light which ages ago came to this world as its Light, to teach us all to say at the end of our earthly pilgrimage here, as He said at the close of His: "Father, into thy hands I commend my spirit."

WAY OF THE CROSS
FOR COMMUNISTS

Address delivered on April 15, 1938

FIRST STATION
Jesus is condemned to Death.

Nineteen hundred years ago Pilate condemned Jesus to death on three false charges: because He was perverting the nation, because He refused to give tribute to Caesar, and because He called Himself a King.

The modern Pilates in Mexico, Germany, Russia, and Red Spain condemn Him to the cross on exactly the same false charges. The Caesar that set himself up as the judge of God then, is today setting himself up as the judge of His Church and His people. Thus it is that today as yesterday the words of the Creed ring true: Jesus Christ is still "suffering under Pontius Pilate".

✦   ✦   ✦

O Jesus, by Thy submission to the unjust judgments of these new Pilates, Thou dost teach us that the State, jealous of Thy Divine Power will be the last enemy of Thy Church. But, in Thy Mercy, grant these States, even at the moment they condemn us, an understanding of what Thou didst tell Pilate: "There is no power but from God." But let us also see the more sad and tragic truth, that if we who profess to be Thy Disciples had

*lived more by Thy Love these very States would want less to
live by hate and to crucify.*

SECOND STATION
Jesus takes His Cross.

Not even Divine Innocence escaped a cross. Why then should
human sinfulness ever hope to escape it? The Son of God came
to earth to revolutionize it by love, but His revolution meant not
violence to one's neighbor, his property, his rights, his religion,
but rather violence to ourselves, our selfishness, our egotisms,
our injustices, and our greed.

✦   ✦   ✦

*Dear Savior, Thy Cross is a reminder that nothing will ever be
perfect here below—not even after a revolution. The greatest
cross mankind can carry is the desire to build an order without
the cross. The sickle and the hammer mean we have no other
destiny than to cut grass and pound iron, but Thy Cross means
that when we have reaped our harvests and beaten plough
shares into swords we must be so unselfish as to be ready to
lay down our lives for our fellowmen—even for those who
give us our cross.*

THIRD STATION
Jesus falls the First time.

The burden of the world's deceit was too great and Jesus falls for
the first time under its weight. Men worshiped Him with her
lips, but their hearts were far from Him. Judas dipped his hand
in the dish in token of friendship, went out into the night, sold
Him for thirty pieces of silver, and in response to the salutation,

"Friend", blistered His lips with a kiss and delivered Him over
to enemies.

✦   ✦   ✦

In this very hour, dear Jesus, there are those who say they
would not burn Thy tabernacles, murder Thy people, nor
desecrate Thy sacred Presence. But these words are like the
kiss of Judas, a gesture of people until they are strong enough
for war; a breaking of bread at our table until they can steal
our bread. Holy Savior, by this Thy first fall, teach us to call
them Friends even when they deceive, that all the world may
know we live by love, even when we fall by their deceit.

Fourth Station
Jesus meets his Blessed Mother.

In the world's new Calvary where Jesus goes out to be re-cru-
cified, it is the family which suffers most. The revolutionary
spirit would make the worker and not the parents the unit of
the new society, and the children the property of the State. Even
in this hour its new commandment rings out: Honor not thy
father and thy mother, but honor the dictator from whom the
father and the mother derive their rights.

✦   ✦   ✦

Mary, Immaculate Mother, thou didst protest against Caesar's
unjust invasion of thy parental rights by stationing thyself on
the road to Calvary to embrace thy Sorrowful Son, and to
declare to all the world that thou wert still His Mother. Do thou
now inspire all Christian mothers to glory in their motherhood
even when Caesar would say they were only nurses. Thou

didst raise thy Son to be a laborer, but thou didst also raise
Him to be a Redeemer. Workers, then, need not be atheists,
for thy Worker was the Son of God; but mothers must always
be mothers, even if they have to claim their children as they
march through the door of death to meet their God.

Fifth Station
Simon of Cyrene helps Jesus.

Bloodshed and revolution though inspired by leaders are not
always executed by them. Rather do these leaders incite the mob
to carry out their nefarious designs. As it is now, so it was on
the first Way of the Cross. Fearful lest Jesus might die on the
way, and thus deprive them of the brutal thrill of crucifixion,
His enemies pushed out of the mob a carpenter by the name of
Simon of Cyrene, whom they forced to help Jesus carry His Cross.

✦ ✦ ✦

Divine Redeemer, before Simon saw Thee face to face he
believed the evil Thy enemies had spoken against Thee, but
once he came close enough to know Thee he began to love
Thee. Thus Thou didst teach the masses of this day that it is
only ignorance of religion that makes men hate religion, and
that in Thee alone will workers find their true Friend, for it
was on the road to Calvary that Simon the carpenter met the
Carpenter of the Universe.

Sixth Station
Veronica wipes the face of Jesus.

Human beings were not all meant to carry either a sickle or a
hammer. Some are meant to carry towels—to wipe away the

beads of feverish brows, to stroke the aching head, and to touch the worn face as with healing wings. Such was the mission of Veronica, who dared brave a violent mob to refresh the Savior and in reward to receive on her towel the imprint of the Face that saved the World.

✦   ✦   ✦

By that miracle, Thou didst testify, Divine Savior, that society has a place not only for toilers but also for mourners, whose delicate sympathies lighten the burden of those who also must carry a cross. Grant unto the world which is rapidly becoming so violent, an army of Veronicas to wipe away the tears of the victims of violence; and do Thou also let them see that when they do it to the least of their brethren they, like Veronica of old, do it unto Thee.

Seventh Station
Jesus falls the second time.

The first fall was from the world's deceit: the second was from the world's injustice. Not one of the four judges proved his case against Our Lord, nor could they agree on the charges. Before two of the judges He was accused of blaspheming God, and before two others He was accused of betraying Caesar. Such gross injustice was too much for the Heart of Justice, and under this weight He fell with His Cross a second time.

✦   ✦   ✦

Even in this day Thou dost fall again under the weight of the world's injustice. Thy enemies cannot agree why Thou shouldst be condemned, they can only agree on condemnation. Like

Pilate and Herod, nations which are political enemies become friends only over Thy torn and bleeding Body. Through Thy rising after the second fall, teach us that Truth crushed to earth will rise again. Inspire us to preach unto death the double piety to God and country! To render unto Caesar the things that are Caesar's, and to God the things that are God's.

EIGHTH STATION
Jesus meets the women of Jerusalem.

Along sorrow's trail consoling women wept at the sight of a Man with a Cross. But to Jesus that was just their mistake: the greatest evil to them was *pain*; to Him it was *sin*. That is why He turned to them and said: Weep not over me; but weep for yourselves, and for your children"; that is, weep for the next generation who come after you, who will bear the accumulated burden of guilt. Shed no tears for My wounded Body, but shed tears for the sin which made these wounds possible.

✦   ✦   ✦

How we need that lesson today. Round about us, Merciful Redeemer, are those who weep over the economic, political, and financial failures, as the women wept over Thy wounds. Speak to them as Thou didst speak to the women of Jerusalem and remind them that our ills are not so much economic and political as moral and religious, and that if we had sinned less we would have been troubled less. Remind our false reformers that property is not the cause of our ills, but rather the greed of those who own, and the envy of those who want to own. Let us weep for sin and then we shall not have to weep for pain.

NINTH STATION
Jesus falls the third time.

Deceit caused the first fall, injustice the second; but the last of all crosses to fall upon the shoulders of Jesus was the cross of persecution. The constant beatings of the executioners, the piercing burning of the crown of thorns, the flowing rivulets of open wounds, brought Jesus for the third time to the earth he had made.

✦   ✦   ✦

We see Thee, Dear Jesus, fall again to the earth today under the weight of the world's violence. Men cannot dethrone Thee in Thy Glory, so they dethrone Thee in Thy Ambassadors. They cannot scale the heavens, so they profane Thy temples, "liquidate" those consecrated to Thy service, and, as Thou hast prophesied, rejoice in their violence as though they had done a service to God. But as Thou didst rise from Thy Third Fall to forgive, so give us strength to rise after a persecution, not to avenge our enemies but to embrace them, for an enemy is conquered only when he is forgiven and loved.

TENTH STATION
Jesus is stripped of His garments.

In those days there were also those who believed in violent dispossession of property, and, in order that even that injustice would be visited upon the Poor Man of Galilee, the executioners stripped Him of His garments—the last vestige of privacy and liberty. The courts had robbed Him of His rights, and now the mob robbed Him of His clothes. Naked He stands, without any possession; and still He is hated.

✦   ✦   ✦

Thus Thou didst teach us, O Savior, that Thy followers will be hated, not only when they possess, but even when they are dispossessed. Even those with vows of poverty will be hunted as Thou, Poverty Itself, wert crucified. But give us strength to see that even though they take away what we have, we still have left, like Thee, the greatest possession of all which no man can take away, namely, what we are—Thy Property, Thy Possession.

Eleventh Station
Jesus is nailed to the Cross.

The sickle mowed down the weeds on Calvary's hill and the hammer drove the nails, and above both was unfurled the Banner of the world's salvation Whose First Word from the Cross was a prayer for the wielders of the sickle and the drivers of the hammer: "Father, forgive them, for they know not what they do."

✦   ✦   ✦

Does that mean, dear Jesus, that we must forgive even the Communists who drove Thee out of Russia, massacred Thy religious in Spain, and closed Thy Churches in Mexico? Thy words can mean nothing else, for on another mount we heard Thee say: "Do good to them that hate you." It will be hard, dear Jesus, but make it easy tor us to forgive by seeing, as Thou dost see so clearly that they know not what they do. We do forgive them, for if we had wrongly believed all the evil they did about Thee, we would probably have done worse!

TWELFTH STATION
Jesus dies on the Cross.

Religion, they say, is the opium of the people, because it teaches that man need not be concerned with economic injustices because there is a future life wherein these injustices are righted. The answer to that lie was given this hour when Jesus refused the opium offered Him on the Cross, so that He ... might surrender His life in full possession of His faculties for the redemption of men who were *still living in this world* and would *live in it until the crack of doom.*

✦ ✦ ✦

Thy religion, O Redeemer of the human race, instead of making this world unimportant makes it all-important, for didst Thou not leave heaven for earth and eternity for time? Didst Thou not say that if we are unjust here below that happiness will be denied us hereafter, and that if we live only for what we can amass here below even that little shall be taken away? Thou hast made this world of so much value that by loving the poor in it and forgiving our enemies we can exchange it for another world where there is Peace because there is Love.

THIRTEENTH STATION
Jesus is taken down from the Cross.

For the perfect, the end is always the same as the beginning. Fittingly, then, when Jesus finishes the work given Him to do, and commends His soul to His Heavenly Father, He is taken down from the Cross and laid in the arms of His Blessed Mother. It was from there He began to run His course, and now that it is finished, He goes back again to that same embrace.

✦   ✦   ✦

Dear Mother of Jesus, as we contemplate Him white in Bethlehem as He came from God, and now red on Calvary as He came from us, we cannot help but see that children belong primarily to mothers and not to the State. The power which crucified has forgotten Him now, but not the Mother who gave Him birth. Hold thy Son close to thy breast and let the world see that only mothers really care. By that love preserve all children under thy protection in order that all the world may love the mother with a cradle more than the woman with a hammer.

Fourteenth Station
Jesus is laid in the Sepulchre.

It was a rich man who gave Jesus a sepulcher, for having heard Our Lord say, "Woe to you that are rich", he understood that riches are given by God to be used in stewardship. Into that tomb Our Lord is laid for the first kind of embrace the earth gave Him since the day of His Birth. The tomb was sealed, soldiers were set on guard, and the enemies rejoiced at their victory: Religion was crushed and would never rise again.

✦   ✦   ✦

O God, how foolish are the ways of Thy enemies! Ten thousand times since that day they have sealed Thy tomb and each time Thou hast burst forth in the glory of Thy Resurrection. Rome buried Thee under ten persecutions, but Thou didst rise to convert Europe. Russia now has her Good Friday of seeming victory, but she may be within three days of her redemption and her peace. We do not ask Thee to condemn our enemies:

we pray Thee to bless them, for we too have been Thine enemies because we hated. Make us all to rise above class struggle and hatred, above that world where we call merely one class "Comrade", unto that greater unity of love wherein we shall call God "Our Father," Thee "Our Brother," the Holy Ghost "Our Sanctifier," and Mary "Our Mother."

THE TWO
REVOLUTIONS

Address delivered on April 17, 1938

Our Lord remade the world by reforming man. This is the lesson of Easter day, so contradictory to the spirit of the world which reforms institutions but leaves man unreformed. Must man rise to a new life before the world can be reborn, or must the institutions of the world be first remade and then man will be remade? That is the problem of Good Friday and it is our problem today. Is social betterment a by-product of better human living, or is the happier human life a product of new politics and renovated economics. More briefly still, which shall we reform first, institutions or man?

The world answers: Reform institutions. Some say, reform private property and men will no longer be selfish: others say, reform parliaments into dictatorships and men will no longer be egotists; others say, reform the monetary system and men will no longer be greedy. In each and every instance the revolution is against something outside of man—his property, his government, his finances; never once is *man* blamed for the world's debacle and never once does the reform touch man.

So insignificant is man in this scheme, that today the tendency is to *make man fit institutions*. Instead of the State existing for man, man exists for the State. As clay is molded in the hands of the potter, so man is de-humanized and de-personalized and then poured into a dictatorial pattern and comes out identified either with a nation, a race, or a class. A governmental policy is worth more than a man. Hence if millions are deprived of liberty, or if hundreds of thousands starve, or if thousands are purged, it matters not as long as the Party survives. Instead of making the hat fit the head, the new reformers make the head fit the hat; which is only another way of saying that institutions, political themes, dictatorships, must survive even though it means the destruction of man.

The Christian reform is just the opposite. It believes that the reformation must begin in man. It agrees that there should be revolution, but maintains that the revolution should not be against something *outside* man, but something inside man, namely, his pride, his egotism, his selfishness, his envy, and his avarice. It places the blame not on institutions, but on humanity; not on things, but on persons; not on property, but on man; not on parliaments, but on conscience. Man is always prone to blame someone else; from earliest childhood when he kicked and banged the door because he bumped his nose, to that other childhood when in a game of golf he cursed the demons of hell and the God of heaven because he missed the cup. The ball was not to blame, nor the club, nor the demons of hell, nor the God of heaven; it was the golfer himself who was to blame. The world is like the golfer; always blaming everything except the one thing in which the blame should be placed, namely, man himself.

Transferring blame is no solution. The fault is in man. Hence, what is the use of transferring the title of property from a few selfish individuals to a few selfish bureaucrats, if you still leave both greedy and dishonest? Why blame the tools, when the ruin is caused by the one who misuses them? Why blame parliament, when the actions of parliament are really the actions of the human beings who compose it? Why blame the river for being polluted, when dirty streams flow into it? In other words, remake man and you remake the world and all its institutions.

These two contrasting ideologies met in conflict centuries ago in the time perspective of those three days from Good Friday to Easter Sunday. On one side was Our Lord Who came to preach the necessity of remaking man. He placed the blame for chaos not on money, but on men; not on politics, but on politicians; not on military strategy, but on generals; not on dictatorship, but on dictators; not on money-lending, but on money lenders. All these things had to be revolutionized, but the way to revolutionize them is first to revolutionize man. Therefore He said nothing about slavery, but He said everything about the dignity of man; He said nothing about finances, but everything about the rich men who like Dives luxuriate their way to hell; He said nothing about violence against Capitalism, but everything about violence against the selfishness of the man who lays up treasures which rust consumes and moths eat; He said nothing against armaments, but He said everything against the man who draws his sword in hate. It was man who had to be reborn, to die himself, to take up his daily cross, to cut off his hands of selfishness, to pluck his eyes out of envy, to become as a servant if he were master, to bless if he were persecuted, to forgive if he were reviled, to rejoice if he were hated, and above all else, to die to his lower life, like a seed falling to the ground, that he might live in the newness of a resurrected life where man lives even when the world dies. That is why He left the institutions alone; He left Pilate on his judgment seat, Herod with his court, Annas with his Sanhedrin, soldiers on their streets. Roman money on the custom table, Caesar on his thrown, and chose twelve men whom He remade in His Image and filled with His Spirit, and then sent them out to conquer the world and its institutions.

Naturally, the world which blamed institutions could not tolerate Him Who blamed man. That is why, though they disagreed among themselves, they all agreed that He should die. It was an insult to them to say that they were to blame, just as it would be an insult to many a modern State to say its leaders or its Dictators were selfish and sinful. All the leaders or its Dictators were selfish and sinful. All the Judges agreed that He should die rather than that their institutions should perish, just as today it is agreed that man should die rather than that the Dictatorship perish. They would have proclaimed Him King if He said the fault was in things; but they crucified Him because He said the fault was in man. They would have welcomed Him if He reformed institutions, but they reviled Him because He sought to reform man. Good Friday was the world's answer to God—the temporary triumph of those who make the reformation of institutions more important than the reformation of man. In perfect keeping with the philosophy of subjecting the human to the institutional, the Judges nailed Him to a cross. A man was fitted to a thing; God Incarnate was crucified to a Cross; Divine Life was sacrificed for a policy; a soul was patterned to force. It was like a sick patient killing the physician, because he found the source of the disease.

But by the most peculiar paradox in the history of the world, in crucifying Him they proved that He was right and they were wrong, and by defeating Him they lost the day. In killing Him they transformed Him; by the power of God they changed mortality into Immortality. The cross was the very thing He said a man must carry in order to be remade; they gave Him the Cross, and He turned it into a throne of glory. He said a man must die in order to live; they gave Him death, and He lived anew. He said that unless the seed falling to the ground dies, it remaineth alone; they planted Him as a seed on Friday, and on Easter He rose like the flower breaking through the sod at springtime in the newness of Divine Life. He said that none shall be exalted unless he is humbled; they humbled Him on Calvary, and He became exalted over an empty grave. They sowed His body in dishonor and He rose in glory; they sowed It in weakness and It rose in power. In taking away His life, they gave Him new life. Remake man and you remake the world!

The doors of the upper room were shut when "Jesus stood in the midst of them, and saith to them: Peace *be* to you."[146] "He showed them his hands and his side."[147] He was the same Jesus they knew, the same Man Who was crucified; that is why He showed them Hands that had busied themselves with His Father's business, Hands that had been placed on the heads of little children, Feet that carried Him to mountain tops for all night vigils of prayer, Feet that had hastened to the side of the wretched and stood near the forlorn, Feet that had failed Him in Gethsemane under a load of sorrow, a Side that was whole as John leaned against it to hear the very secrets of the Heart of God, a Side that John a little later saw opened with a lance that Love might stand revealed, and that like another open door in another Noah's ark all men might enter for escape from the flood of sin. He was the same Man, and yet He was different, for He now came to them through closed doors. The death marks proved His relation to the Cross, but they also proved His power over it, for wounds are now scars to prove that Love is stronger than death. It was no ghost the Apostles were seeing, despite His entrance through closed doors and despite His celestial radiance and the Glory of His Resurrection. He had lived the Gospel He had preached: The way to reform the world is to reform man.

---

[146] Luke 24:36.

[147] John 20:20.

Within forty years after, the world that put Him to death was dead; but He lives on. And thus there emerges from Easter the lesson: Reform man and you remake the world.

A dozen times in history this lesson has been repeated. First of all, when Peter and Paul went out to preach the Gospel of the Resurrection and the paganism of the Roman Empire answered with persecution. It refused to believe that pagan man needed reformation. In order to better show its belief in the subjection of man to institutions, it fitted the Christians to Caesar's rack as it had fitted Christ to Caesar's Cross. There must have been those who believed that the way to save Christianity was to reform the Roman Empire—but not the Apostles! They had the mandate from their Master to regenerate man. Instead of preaching revolution against Caesar, they preached revolution against sin. Instead of attacking the indignities of Roman citizenship they preached the glories of the citizenship of the saints in the Kingdom of God. Instead of attacking pagan gods, they preached that the God Who enthrones Himself by grace in the soul was not made by hands; instead of changing institutions they changed man. And even while Peter and Paul stood by their graves already dug, a new world of Truth and Love arose. Paganism crumbled into the dust of its earthen gods, as once more the Easter lesson was proclaimed: Reform man, and you remake the world!

Then came the Church's conflict with the institution of slavery, in which man was a chattel and a piece of merchandise like the grain he sold. Never once did the Church preach a revolution against slave-owners; but unceasingly did it preach the inherent dignity of man, that each man, because endowed with an immortal soul, is possessed of inalienable rights which no State or Master can take away. St. Paul wrote to a slave owner asking him to take back a slave, but to remember that the slave, now baptized, was a child of God and an heir of heaven. Under the influence of the Church, Constantine and Justinian passed a series of humane laws forbidding the separation of slaves from their families. Later on the Order of Our Lady of Ransom redeemed half a million slaves in four centuries. In 1537 Paul III declared that the natives of America had equal rights before God with their conquerors. Slowly, the Christian ferment of human personality entered society and in 1610 St. Peter Claver landed at Cartagena in the Caribbean Sea, the chief slave market of the world, where slaves were sold in bundles of six. For thirty-eight years St. Peter Claver labored among them, washed them, dressed their wounds, made their beds, and mothered them and preached to them their dignity before God. The institution of slavery died, because the inherent value of man was preached, as once more there rang out over the world the lesson of Easter morn: Reform man and you remake the world!

Can we run counter to history? Shall we waste all our time reforming our politics, our economics, our parliaments, and leave man untouched? Shall we go on pouring ephemeral facts into the minds of our students, and leave their hearts and wills undisciplined? Shall we remake relations between Capital and Labor and do nothing to take envy out of the heart of the laborer, and avarice out of the heart of the Capitalist? Shall we seek international peace by reforming agreements, pacts, and treaties, or by reforming man into a consciousness of his brotherhood with Christ under the Fatherhood of God?

I am not saying that political, economic, and social reforms are unimportant; I am only saying they are secondary to the reformation of man, for social amelioration is a by-product of God-like living. If there were any other way to build a Christian civilization than by the Crucifixion, Our Lord would have chosen it; if there were any other exit from an empty tomb than through the door of the Cross, Our Lord would have passed through it; if there were any other way to have all things added to us than seeking first the Kingdom of God and His Justice, Our Lord would never have commanded it. We are merely scratching the surface of the world's ills, covering the world's prejudice with face powder, soothing national concerns with alcohol rubs, changing our title to property without uprooting selfishness. Very simply, unless man is reformed, the world will never be remade for there is no escaping the Easter lesson: Reform man and you remake the world!

Choose your revolution! A Revolution there must be. The Revolution of Institutions or the Revolution of Man; the Spirit of Revolution or the Revolution of Spirit; violence against our neighbor or violence against ourselves; revolt against institutions or revolt against our passions, for the lesson of Easter morn is inescapable: Reform man, and you remake the world. If you choose to reform institutions you will have a tremendous following—you will have in your retinue the race of those who throw away their tools because they clumsily pinched their fingers; you will be called a Liberator by men, because you still leave them free to be selfish, mean, and base: you will be called a great Progressive because you will still allow the robbers to rob, the thieves to steal, and the agitators to agitate. But you will never remake the world, for you did not reform yourself and your following will be the following of death, for *the world and its concupiscence die*; only by a Resurrection does man live.

But if you reform yourself, do violence to yourself and not to your neighbor, do violence to your envy and not to his home, do violence to your avarice and not to his family, do violence to your sin and not to his shop, you may not be acclaimed by the mobs, you may even be crucified for your faith, but you will do more to remake the world than all the superficial reformers of institutions; and your following will be the following of Divine Life, for you will have rescued from this earth the one thing Christ rescued from it—the immortality of a resurrected man.

Let themes crackle and go up in smoke! Let enslaving tyrants bomb their way to proletarian thrones and be delivered to mummification. But keep your soul your own and you will walk with the Risen Christ in the glory of the Eternal hills. For it is to the saving of man by spiritual regeneration that Easter calls us; that is why true Christianity is the greatest revolution in the world. It is easy to topple thrones; it is easy to burn palaces; it is easy to shout "down with classes"; it is easy to destroy civilization—these revolutions only touch the surface of things. But to topple selfishness, bomb greed, destroy sin—that requires the heroism of burying your lower self in the Calvary of Christian mortification to live the renewed Christ-life. That will make you one of the greatest revolutionists in the world—a saint!

Whichever revolution you choose will have its symbol. Either the clenched fist of Good Friday or the folded hands of Easter. If you wan to reform institutions and forget about your own need of reformation, you will choose the symbol of the clenched fist. The clenched fist—the symbol of hatred and bitterness; the symbol of the burning tabernacles, the pillages homes, the desecrated corpses; the symbol of that which tears down and has nothing to put in its place; the symbol of that which strikes the neighbor; the one gesture that turns the hand of man which was meant to be an instrument of art into that which most closely resembles the claw of a beast.

The other symbol of those who believe in the internal revolution against baseness and the need of regeneration from on high, is that of the folded hands of Easter morn. Folded hands cannot strike, for they were not made for offense; they cannot protect, for they were not made for defense; they can only supplicate, only pray: ten Gothic spires—a carnal decade aspiring heavenward in petition for the souls of men.

And by and through those folded hands may all the race of the clenched fists—the race of Cain—come to the side of an Empty tomb, where stands Christ with scarred hands and feet, dug with the hammer of hate; and by and through the charities and prayers of folded hands, may those clenched fists, as it were, *open* and release their hate. And then those hands which were nailed by hate will lift themselves and fold together, not in Judgment, but in the embrace of Easter, that all the world may know—how sweet is the Love of Christ!

⚖️ AFTERWORD

Richard Aleman

The re-emergence of Ven. Fulton Sheen's *Justice and Charity* arrives on the heels of rousing debates amongst Catholics about the Church's social thought. This is especially so in the age of Pope Francis, who, following in the footsteps of his predecessors, is shining a light on the importance of living out the two great commandments in society, in politics, and in economic life. Indeed, the divisions between Left and Right, within and outside of the Church, have left many people feeling intellectually homeless and pinned between the prevailing schools of social or economic libertarianism. God willing, this title will provoke serious contemplation in the mind of honest readers willing to be led by the mind of the Church, guided by one of Catholicism's most erudite spokesmen.

Fulton Sheen's vocation and career in broadcasting made him a household name, from his "Catholic Hour" radio broadcasts to his successful television programs. Although the "Life is Worth Living" star always steered his audience in the direction of his great love, Jesus Christ, Sheen often quoted a person who had an indelible mark on his career: the English writer G.K. Chesterton.[148] It may surprise many to know the two men actually met. When this meeting took place may be difficult to pinpoint exactly, but it was in the early 1920s, perhaps when

---

[148] Fulton J. Sheen, *Treasures in Clay: The Autobiography of Fulton J. Sheen* (New York: Doubleday, 2008).

Sheen served as the unofficial curate of St. Patrick's in Soho. He crossed the hustle and bustle of Fleet Street and knocked on the door of Chesterton's London office, asking the famous writer to compose an introduction for his doctrinal dissertation, *God and Intelligence in Modern Philosophy: A Critical Study in the Light of the Philosophy of Saint Thomas.*

> "The writer recalls having asked Mr. Chesterton a few years ago to write a preface for a philosophical work which was about to come from the press. Mr. Chesterton objected on the grounds that he knew nothing about philosophy. When the writer retorted that he had written a very excellent philosophy himself, namely, *Orthodoxy*, Mr. Chesterton answered that *Orthodoxy* was only a popular work, whereas the one for which he was asked to write a preface was scientific.
>
> He then leaned back his bulk of weight, both physical and mental, in that rather uncomfortable chair of his newspaper office, and said: 'Yes, I will write the preface. After all, we both belong to that great mystical corporation called the Catholic Church, in which we can stand responsible for one another's opinions. I know what you must believe, and you know what I must believe.' In that sentence was an understanding of the Church to which few arrive, even those who are born in it. It was only to be expected then that when Mr. Chesterton decided to wield a pen like a sword in defense of the Church, it would reflect something of that deep understanding of it, and this expectation has been realized in his new book, *The Resurrection of Rome.*"[149]

While teaching at Catholic University of America in Washington, D.C., Sheen returned to England in 1936 on the

---

[149] Fulton J. Sheen, "The Conqueror of Death," *The Commonweal* (Feb. 18, 1931).

solemn occasion of Chesterton's death, a man so beloved by its people that Pope Pius XI famously sent a consoling telegram to the nation of England acknowledging this loss. Attending the requiem held at Westminster Cathedral, the middle-aged Sheen shared its pews with the English writer's most distinguished acquaintances and treasured friends: Hilaire Belloc, biographer Maisie Ward, her husband and apologist Frank Sheed, the poet Walter de la Mare, the renowned Fr. C.C. Martindale, Aldous Huxley, and many more. Fr. John O'Connor—the inspiration for Chesterton's fictional priest detective, Father Brown—chanted the Mass, and Fr. Vincent McNabb, the celebrated Dominican friar and loyal ally of Chesterton, served as sub-deacon.

None other than Fr. Ronald Knox delivered the sermon on that gloomy day, cautioning the world against neglecting Chesterton's gift to the world.[150] For a short time, the world did ignore Chesterton, who was eclipsed by his secularly attractive friends George Bernard Shaw and H.G. Wells. Only a handful of scholars and friends saved Chesterton's thought from exile, and Sheen was one of them.

> "Long before Chesterton saw that flash of the lightening which was the Light amongst men, he bore a keen admiration for the Church. Once that flash had illumined his mind and brought him to the Wisdom which leaves all other wisdom cold, he became a veritable fire of enthusiasm for the Church, which before he knew but did not know that he knew."[151]

---

[150] "If posterity neglects him, it will pronounce judgment not upon him, but upon itself." Ronald A. Knox, *Pastoral Sermons and Occasional Sermons* (San Francisco: Ignatius Press, 2002).

[151] Sheen, "The Conqueror of Death."

Their intellectual kinship and fidelity to Christ's Church was not all they shared. Both Sheen and Chesterton also shared a love of Catholic social thought. It is fitting that only two years after G.K. Chesterton went to his eternal reward, Fulton Sheen delivered his most powerful sermons on Catholic social teaching in a series of talks originally broadcast on his "Catholic Hour" radio program, later published by *Our Sunday Visitor* under the title *Justice and Charity*.

Historically situated at the tail end of Stalin's "Great Purge" to drive out any opposition to the working class in the Soviet Union, this series wasn't his first foray in what would become a lifelong battle against the forces of communism. Even before Sheen became a major player in broadcasting, he was already recruiting for his crusade against Marxism. He played an instrumental role in the notable conversions of ex-Communists such as Douglas A. Hyde, former news editor of London's Communist *Daily Worker*. Sheen helped Hyde turn Communist tactics "into techniques for making converts for Christ."[152] Interestingly, Chesterton also struck a chord in Hyde's political conversion. "My reading of Chesterton, Belloc, and *The Weekly Review*," Hyde wrote in his autobiography, "had convinced me that they were right on fundamentals."[153] Years later, after testifying for the U.S. House Committee on Un-American Activities on communism, and writing many books and articles warning of what lay behind the Iron Curtain, Sheen helped Bella Dodd, author of *School of Darkness* and former member of the Communist Party of America, come to the Church.

---

[152] Sheen, *Treasures in Clay*.

[153] Douglas Hyde, *I Believed: The Autobiography of a Former British Communist* (London: Pan Books, 1961).

Of course, Sheen's virulent rejection of communism did not make the holy priest a spokesperson for capitalism either.[154] Like Chesterton before him, Sheen warned of capitalism's remarkable similarities to communism. Hudge and Gudge—Chesterton's terrific names for "big business" and "big government"— simply meant that "ownership in the hands of a few capitalists [became] ownership in the hands of a few bureaucrats."[155] Without question, Sheen was critical of Marxist-sympathizing priests for their emphasis on politics "without any sanctification or salvation of those in the pews,"[156] but he also held capitalism suspect for its indifference towards religion and its embrace of a world where "no church, no Bible, no moral law [tells] a man what he ought to do with his wealth."[157]

The worship of Venus, wrote Sheen, cheapens marriage and love, but objectifying the dignity of the human person is also tied with our genuflecting in front of Mammon, a combination that intoxicates the poor and the rich alike.[158] This "cocktail" often becomes a source of conflict between owners and workers:

> "To ask which is more important—Capital or Labor—is like asking which is more important to a man, the right leg or the left. Since they both have a common function, they

---

[154] "In *Quadragesimo Anno* Pope Pius XI referred to the liberal theory of uncontrolled competition as a 'poisoned spring' from which have originated all the errors of individualism. The French hierarchy, commenting upon the same pope's letter on communism, stated: By condemning the actions of communist parties, the Church does not support the capitalist regime." National Conference of Catholic Bishops, *Pastoral Letter on Marxist Communism*, 1980.

[155] "Capitalism and Socialism Are Related," *Toledo Blade* (December 9, 1951): 5.

[156] "Forty Percent," *Lewiston Evening Journal* (July 26, 1975).

[157] *Ibid.*

[158] *Ibid.*

should function together. Conflicts between Capital and Labor are wrong, not because they hold up the delivery of goods, but for the moral reason that they create distorted personal relationships, just as the quarrel of a husband and wife disrupts the good of the family."[159]

Few men, like Sheen, have connected the dots that weave together culture, politics, economics, and faith.[160] Our society today views these areas of life as disconnected from each other. Instead, choice is seen as the only legitimate moral act of human freedom, flowing from "the right," in the words of U.S. Supreme Court Justice Anthony Kennedy, "to define one's own concept of existence, of meaning, of the universe, and of the mystery of human life."[161]

The moral crisis at the heart of our current social and economic imbalances is a reminder of the war being waged between the pernicious powers of this world and the followers of Christ. Many see institutional change as needed to correct social injustice, as rightly they should. Yet as necessary as systemic changes may be in correcting systemic problems, Sheen emphasizes that only by remaking man can we remake the world:

> [The world] will not rise to peace and happiness through economic and political remedies alone: it will rise only through a spiritual regeneration of the hearts and souls of men.... It

---

[159] Fulton J. Sheen, *Philosophies at War* (New York: Charles Scribner's Sons, 1943).

[160] "For, it is the opinion of some, and the error is already very common, that the social question is merely an economic one, whereas in point of fact it is, above all, a moral and religious matter, and for that reason must be settled by the principles of morality and according to the dictates of religion." Leo XIII, *Graves de communi re*, no. 11.

[161] *Planned Parenthood v. Casey*, 505 U.S. 833 (1992).

will not be saved by social recovery but by rebirth—rebirth from the dead by the Power of Divinity in Christ.[162]

Critics may say this work is dated, that communism has failed and the market prevailed, but one look at our present realities may turn this supposition on its head. Not only are the fundamental truths in this book appropriate for discerning what causes societal dysfunction at all levels, but they also show how to tread through the muck of ideologies alien to the teachings of the Church. *Justice and Charity* is a full-bodied introduction to the social doctrine of the Church desperately needed now, when we must rehabilitate this formative part of our Catholic education and loosen the grip of the dominant paradigm of Left and Right, which has such a hold over the minds of laymen and clergy alike.

In life, and in death, Fulton Sheen and Gilbert K. Chesterton continue to be remembered as faithful sons of the Church, instruments of conversion for men and women from all walks of life, not only in their time, but today as well. Only a force as powerful as God's will could have endowed these colossal men with their gift of communicating the faith. Their intellectual breadth was matched by their generosity, their love of wonder, of the poor, and God.

Ven. Fulton Sheen is a shining example for Christians around the world. As St. John Paul II wrote on the occasion of Sheen's sixtieth anniversary as a priest, "in these six decades of your priestly service, God has touched the lives of millions of the men and women of our time." With this volume we are pleased to add to his great legacy, and to remind the world that Sheen also understood the importance of G.K. Chesterton and the fullness of Catholic social teaching.

---

[162] Fulton J. Sheen, "No Reason for Despair," *Ottawa Citizen* (Apr. 4, 1950).

TAN · BOOKS

TAN Books is the Publisher You Can Trust With Your Faith.

TAN Books was founded in 1967 to preserve the spiritual, intellectual, and liturgical traditions of the Catholic Church. At a critical moment in history TAN kept alive the great classics of the Faith and drew many to the Church. In 2008 TAN was acquired by Saint Benedict Press. Today TAN continues to teach and defend the Faith to a new generation of readers.

TAN publishes more than 600 booklets, Bibles, and books. Popular subject areas include theology and doctrine, prayer and the supernatural, history, biography, and the lives of the saints. TAN's line of educational and homeschooling resources is featured at TANHomeschool.com.

TAN publishes under several imprints, including TAN, Neumann Press, ACS Books, and the Confraternity of the Precious Blood. Sister imprints include Saint Benedict Press, Catholic Courses, and Catholic Scripture Study.

**For more information about TAN,
or to request a free catalog, visit
TANBooks.com**

**Or call us toll-free at
(800) 437-5876**